The War On Whites

How Hating White People Became the New National Sport

Ed Brodow

The War on Whites

*How Hating White People
Became the New National Sport*

Published by Ed Brodow/TousDroit Publishing
ed@brodow.com
www.edbrodowpolitics.com

Cover Design by Dawn Zirlilight

Contents

Also by Ed Brodow

America on its Knees
Tyranny of the Minority
Trump's Turn
In Lies We Trust
Negotiation Boot Camp
Beating the Success Trap
Fixer
Women from Venus
Negotiate with Confidence

Introduction: *White Is a Color Too*

Throughout most of recorded history, majorities have oppressed vulnerable minorities. Not the other way around. Jews didn't oppress the majority Christian population in Nazi Germany. Armenians didn't oppress the majority Turkish population. Minority Tutsi did not oppress majority Hutu in Rwanda. That would run counter to common sense.

Yet the modern world offers examples that defy what we would expect from common sense. During the Russian Revolution, the Bolsheviks were a minority that imposed their worldview on the majority of Russians. In contemporary America, minorities are attempting to oppress the majority white population. Under the guise of ending alleged racial oppression, an effort is being made to remake whites into the new underclass. This runs contrary to common sense, but there it is.

Whites are being demonized and marginalized at every turn. Any attempt to say, "I am proud to be white," is met with scorn and ridicule. As a defense against this racist behavior, I have become an advocate for white people. Thirty years ago, this never would have occurred to me. Things have changed. Now when I defend white Americans, I am not referring to white supremacy, whatever that is, and I am not suggesting that whites are better than any other group. I am promoting the excellent value system created by white Americans: respect for the individual, freedom of speech, the rule of law, meritocracy, the work ethic, equality of opportunity, taking personal responsibility, the importance of education. I am lauding the achievements of white people, especially white men, throughout our history.

The white population is not being given credit for its contributions. White men founded our republic. White men ended slavery. Whites are largely responsible for the day-to-day commerce that puts food on the table and clothing on our backs. Like it or not, white people drive the engine that makes our country work. Their track record hasn't been perfect, but their values stand as a role-model for the world.

With the civil rights legislation of the 1960s, whites made it possible for blacks and other minorities to become full partners in the American Dream. "White power" was unchallenged up to that time—yet willingly, unilaterally, they relinquished it. No one forced them to do these things. They acted because it was the right thing to do. What are they getting in return? Contempt, hatred, and intolerance.

The war on whites is un-American. Discrimination against whites is just as bad as discrimination against blacks or anyone else. It is time to declare that white people are victimized by racism and entitled to government protection as much as any other group.

Progressives, writes David Horowitz in *Big Agenda*, are using a politically correct term—*people of color*—to "isolate the white European American majority as an oppressor of everyone else." As a white person who has oppressed no one, I am appalled that my skin color is not considered a color. America needs to be reminded that *white is a color too!*

Ed Brodow
Monterey, California

Chapter One

The Inquisition Against White People

America is more divided than any time since the Vietnam War. There is the political divide between liberals and conservatives, and then there is the issue of race. A racial inquisition aimed at whites is underway based on the erroneous notion that the number one threat to America is ingrained intolerance by white people.

The Left, says author Ben Shapiro, wants to portray America as "an incurable mass of bigoted whites." Colin Flaherty, in *Don't Make the Black Kids Angry: The Hoax of Black Victimization and Those Who Enable It*, refers to this as "the Big Lie: the war on black people and how racist white people are waging it. That is the biggest lie of our generation." President Biden bought into this lie when he said that white supremacy is the number one threat to the nation.

We have reached the point where no one likes white people. It's not just "people of color." Even white people dislike white people. There is open season on whites and, strange as it may seem, large segments of the white population are all for it. "Being white carries so much of a social stigma that it results in job discrimination and more," writes Robert Spencer in *PJMedia*. "Today, to be white is to be evil."

"Anti-white discrimination has become almost an institutional requirement," said Lynn Uzzell in *RealClearPolitics*. "Schools and businesses seem fearful lest they are accused of not doing enough to stereotype, denigrate, marginalize, and suppress 'whiteness.'"

Anti-white hate is an offshoot of the Left's preoccupation with its perverted version of "diversity," where Americans are divided between alleged oppressors—heterosexual, white, Christian males—and victimized groups of minorities and women. Minority groups are said to need protection because they are oppressed by the white majority. This is the victimhood culture of today's college campus, says Scott Greer in *No Campus for White Men: The Transformation of Higher Education into Hateful Indoctrination*, where whites are morally inferior and blacks are superior because of their presumed history of oppression.

Oppressor and victim. "It is the old Marxist wine in new bottles," says David Horowitz in *Big Agenda*, "and the results are bound to be similar."

The prosperity of white Americans is the result of working hard and working smart, not from oppressing others. There was a time in my experience when it was different. I remember visiting Miami, Florida, as a boy and being shocked by the separate drinking fountains at Woolworth's: "white" and "colored." Blacks were forbidden to drink out of the white fountain. At seven years of age, this made no sense to me so I began drinking out of the colored fountain. An older white girl ran over and said, "Little boy, don't drink out of that!" I was terrified that I would become ill. My mother explained that we were now in the South, so I

THE WAR ON WHITES

THE WAR ON WHITES

should expect things to be different from our home in Brooklyn. I will never forget the experience and what it taught me about human foibles.

That kind of anti-black racism is gone from the US. We may be seeing separate drinking fountains again—only this time whites will be targeted for exclusion from the fountain reserved for people of color. Racial bullying is now aimed at white people. I want to be allowed to drink from the same water fountain as the next person. Don't you?

Exterminating White People

Trashing whites is the modus operandi of the Democratic Party. Showing contempt for a half century of enlightened racial tolerance, Democrats—with the support of academia and the media—are trying to divide America along racial lines. Progressive liberals and Democrats, David Horowitz explains in *The Enemy Within*, believe that "what is wrong with America is that there are too many white males occupying positions of power and influence and, allegedly, keeping diverse, 'marginalized,' and 'under-served,' minorities 'in their place.'"

Is that true? Is there a valid argument for putting down white people? The answer—loud and clear—is NO!

In the pre-Obama period, outbursts of anti-white racism were limited to extremists such as Louis Farrakhan and Rev. Jeremiah Wright. In post-Obama America, signs of the inquisition are popping up everywhere. Consider these expressions of anti-white hatred:

5

- Dr. Kamau Kambon, an African-American professor at North Carolina State, told a panel at Howard University Law School, "We have to exterminate white people off the face of the planet."
- Nikole Hannah-Jones, who created the 1619 Project, has alleged that, "The white race is the biggest murderer, rapist, pillager, and thief of the modern world."
- Dr. Donald Moss, a psychoanalyst who teaches at the New York Psychoanalytic Institute, referred to "whiteness" as a "malignant, parasitic-like condition to which white people have a particular susceptibility."
- *New York Times* editorial board member Sarah Jeong tweeted "cancel white people," "white men are bullshit," and "dumbass f---ing white people."
- Lori Lightfoot, when she was mayor of Chicago, announced that she would not be granting interviews to white reporters.
- Psychiatrist Aruna Khilanani told an audience at Yale School of Medicine that she has fantasies of killing whites.
- President Joe Biden urged the graduating class at Howard University to "stand up against the poison of white supremacy ... the most dangerous terrorist threat to our homeland."

These people have not been called to account for their anti-white racism. If the tables were reversed, and hateful comments like these were aimed at black people, the perpetrators would be ostracized and riots would ensue.

Here is a more subtle example of white bashing that may surprise you. "During the 2016 presidential campaign," said African-American economist Walter Williams, "candidate Hillary Clinton claimed that half of Donald Trump's supporters were 'a basket of deplorables' who were 'racist, sexist, homophobic, xenophobic, Islamophobic—you name it.' Do you think Clinton was talking about Trump's black, Asian, and Hispanic supporters? No, *she was talking about millions of Trump's white supporters.*"

Trump aide Stephen Miller has accused President Biden of "racism against white people" and "anti-white bigotry." Miller asks, "When did racism against white people become okay?" He cites examples, including: "Joe Biden put white people last in line for Covid relief funds" and "Progressive corporations, airlines, and universities all openly discriminate against white Americans."

"If everyone knows that treating ethnic and racial minorities as stereotypes is disrespectful, mean-spirited and divisive," wrote Esther Cepeda in the *Washington Post*, "why is it OK when it comes to whites?" It is not okay, but it is happening anyway. It comes as no surprise to anyone who has been watching current social trends.

Thomas Sowell has a penetrating observation in *Wealth, Poverty and Politics* that groups in all cultures exhibit resentment against those in a noticeably successful position, who must be brought down. Usually, Sowell says, it takes the form of a majority that resents a successful minority. But in our case, he observes, the minorities that lag behind are conducting a witch hunt against the successful white majority.

We should be able to accommodate the rights of our minorities without depriving the majority of theirs.

Obama's Racist Legacy

According to Gallup, the percentage of Americans who agree that black-white relations are good is at a 20-year low. It all began with Barack Obama. Different racial and ethnic groups were getting along just fine until 2008. Then Obama showed up and racial division was reintroduced into American life. Instead of recognizing the significance of having a black president, the US has been plagued with an epidemic of racial conflict. Obama's inflammatory statements, one after another, fomented animosity between races. Accusations of white privilege and white supremacy have monopolized our civil discourse.

When police in Cambridge, Massachusetts, arrested African-American Harvard Professor Henry Louis Gates, Obama intervened, saying that the police "acted stupidly." According to *Reuters*, Obama "plunged his presidency into a charged racial debate and set off a firestorm with police officers nationwide by siding with a prominent black scholar who accuses police of racism." Online polls in Massachusetts, it turned out, showed strong support for the white arresting officer. "[Obama] has alienated public safety officers across the country with his comments," said David Holway, president of the International Brotherhood of Police Officers.

Obama later admitted that he had acted poorly in a racially charged case. But the harm was already done. The public was duped by the liberal canard, implied by the president, that white police are out to get black men. Obama and Attorney General Eric Holder continued to imply that black men are dying at the hands of oppressive racist cops. The media ran with it. The gullible public bought it.

After the shooting of Trayvon Martin, a black teenager with a history of violent behavior, Obama inflamed racial hostility among blacks by saying, "If I had a son, he'd look like Trayvon." Once again, thanks to the president's poorly timed comment, we were manipulated into believing that the black perpetrator was the victim and the white defender was the felon.

While addressing a group of police at a slain officer's funeral, Obama made this insensitive statement implying that racist police continue to abuse black criminals: "We know that centuries of racial discrimination, of slavery, and subjugation, and Jim Crow didn't simply vanish with the law against segregation. We know that bias remains."

For the entire term of his presidency, Obama tried unsuccessfully to hide his racist views from the public. In a revealing *CNN* interview, Obama griped that white people are angry because they have to share the country with non-whites. He thinks that if whites refuse to accept race bashing, that makes them racists. If they don't prostrate themselves before critical race theory, he believes, it is because they are afraid of black and brown population growth. Whites should be happy to comply with the inquisition that CRT is mobilizing against them. They should simply take their medicine and shut up. Thank you, Mr. Obama.

Now we know how Obama really feels about the nation that embraced him for eight years. We know without a doubt that he hates America and its white inhabitants. Obama bears "the lion's share of responsibility" for the virulent anti-white racism that reared its ugly head during his tenure, said Ted Nugent on *Real America's Voice.* "He literally reignited racism in America." Post-Obama, said Chris Donaldson in *BizPacReview*, anti-white hate "has since metastasized like a cancer throughout every institution in America."

Obama and his ideological heirs believe that the US is a racist country run by a cabal of immoral white people. To correct this perceived abuse, they want the destruction of all existing political, economic, and social institutions. The Left wants to replace our country with an authoritarian socialist nation run by unaccountable Washington bureaucrats—the Deep State.

"Leftists want you to think America is evil, a horribly racist nation that oppresses everyone except straight white men," said Aaron Kliegman, politics reporter for *Fox News Digital.* "And anyone who defends, let alone celebrates, our country is complicit in the oppression. To the Left," says Kliegman, "America is something to hate, not love, and being American is a source of shame, not pride."

Undoing Your Whiteness—the Newest Cult

Government agencies have bought into the anti-white agenda. Seattle, for example, has inaugurated its own racial inquisition aimed at white people. The city's Office of Civil Rights is holding a segregated training session for white city employees that will train them to "undo their whiteness" and affirm their "complicity in racism." Known as *Interrupting Internalized Racial Superiority and Whiteness*, the session's existence was exposed by Christopher F. Rufo, an editor for *City Journal*, and confirmed by Tucker Carlson on his Fox TV show.

An email to white Seattle city workers demanded that they examine their "complicity in the system of white supremacy." In case any employees were not sure if they should be part of the program, an information sheet described anyone of Arab, Jewish, Finnish, German, Italian, Armenian or Irish descent as white. According to Rufo, white staffers are being informed by their "diversity trainers" that their behavior patterns are rife with "vestiges of internalized racial oppression." Participants are urged to cultivate "networks with other white people who are practicing antiracist accomplicehood so you can talk through your struggles in the work of undoing your own whiteness."

What is it like to be forced to undo your whiteness? What goes on in these training sessions that are popping up everywhere? The invitation to Seattle's program said this: "We'll examine our complicity in the system of white supremacy—how we internalize and reinforce it—and begin to cultivate practices that enable us to interrupt racism in ways to be accountable to Black, Indigenous and People of Color (BIPOC) folks within our community." In other words, you are being coerced into agreeing that if you are white, you are racist—whether you like it or not.

Look at what goes on: The Seattle program demands that its white employees surrender their "physical safety" and "white normative behavior." Trainers instruct white employees in "practicing self-talk that affirms our complicity in racism." Whites are commanded to give up:

- Comfort
- Physical safety
- Control over other people
- Relationships with other white people
- Niceties from neighbors and colleagues
- The certainty of your job
- Accepting jobs and promotions when we are not qualified

A flowchart demonstrated how white people keep the system going by justifying that whites are superior to people of color, arguing that whites have been wronged by people of color, and using anger, self-righteousness, and defensiveness to mask guilt. Whites allegedly internalize their racial superiority using these "white" qualities:

- perfectionism
- individualism
- imposition
- arrogance
- paternalism
- silence
- intellectualization
- control
- violence
- comfort

- appropriation
- cognitive dissonance
- objectivity
- anti-blackness

According to the Seattle program, said Rufo, these qualities "are all vestiges of this internalized racism and must be abandoned in favor of social-justice principles." Jonathan Chait, writing in *New York Magazine*, expanded the list of so-called white values that must be discarded:

- objective, rational thinking
- cause and effect relationships
- hard work is the key to success
- planning for the future
- delayed gratification

"It is the language of cult programming," Rufo said, "persuading members that they are defective in some predefined manner." Rufo refers to the trainings as a "racial justice shakedown" and "the new racial orthodoxy." They have seen exponential growth in the past few years and are sweeping through local government, schools, and corporate HR departments. "Dozens of private firms now offer diversity training to public agencies," Rufo says. "The idea is that all whites have unconscious, 'implicit' bias that they must vigilantly program themselves to overcome, and it has become an article of faith across corporate boardrooms, academe and law enforcement, even though the premise is unscientific and impossible to verify."

ED BRODOW

"It's about hate, humiliation, and power," said Tucker Carlson:

> "It's about hurting people, it always is. Telling people they're inferior because of their skin color was wrong when it happened 60 years ago in Alabama, it is every bit as wrong when it happens today in Seattle or at Yale or Google Headquarters or at your kid's elementary schools. Attacking people on the basis of their race is a sin, there is nothing worse for a country. They can try to disguise it with Orwellian terms like 'anti-racism,' but this is the purest kind of race hate. It will destroy America faster than anything else."

Can you imagine if Seattle required all black employees to undo their blackness? The rioting would go on for weeks. Doing it to white employees, however, is perfectly acceptable. It's hard to believe that anyone would go along with this. We are not living in Nazi Germany.

Seattle has a lot of company. The US Treasury Department held a training session telling employees that "all white people contribute to racism." Sandia National Labs—which produces our nuclear arsenal—held a three-day reeducation camp for white males, teaching them how to deconstruct their "white male culture" and forcing them to write letters of apology to women and people of color. The Department of Homeland Security hosted a training on "microaggressions, microinequities, and microassaults" where white employees were told that they had been "socialized into oppressor roles." Even the FBI's Office of Diversity and Inclusion is hosting weekly Intersectionality Workshops.

Corporate America has joined the fray. A diversity training program at Bank of America teaches that white toddlers "develop racial biases by ages 3-5" and instructs white employees to "cede power to people of color." Google launched an "antiracism" initiative claiming that America is a system of white supremacy and all Americans are "raised to be racist." Defense contractor Raytheon instituted a CRT program that encourages white employees to confront their "privilege," reject the principle of "equality," and "defund the police."

TV commentator John Stossel reported on a Coca-Cola diversity training that urged white participants, "Try to be less white." What did that entail? "To be less white is to: be less oppressive; be less arrogant; be less certain; be less defensive; be less ignorant; be more humble." In other words, it was a vile attack on Coca-Cola's white employees based solely on their skin color.

"Try to be less white," said UK politician Nigel Farage. "The inference here is clear, isn't it? That white is bad; white means supremacist; white means you are guilty!"

"If a company sent around a training kit instructing black people how to 'be less black,'" said black political activist Candace Owens, "the world would implode and lawsuits would follow. I genuinely hope these employees sue Coca-Cola for blatant racism and discrimination."

A twitter user wrote, "Try to be less black. Try to be less Asian. Try to be less Indigenous. Can we say that? No? Then why can Coca Cola tell their staff to be less white?"

"The point is to demonize the other side as much as possible," said former diversity officer Erec Smith. He is correct. The actual purpose of diversity trainings is the demonization of white people. The trainings are examples of racial indoctrination, not racial sensitivity.

Anti-white trainings are big business on campus. In today's universities, says Scott Greer in *No Campus for White Men*, the embracing of identity politics is "increasingly bordering on outright hatred for white people." One of the most popular forms of anti-white discrimination is the indoctrination training forced by many colleges on white freshmen. The purpose, says Greer, is to make whites feel badly about their skin color. Whites should "sit down, shut up, and allow their moral superiors to berate them." Greer cites as an example the "Whiteness" conference at the University of Michigan designed to help white students recognize their alleged privilege.

University of Wisconsin at Madison ran "The Privilege of Whiteness" workshops designed to shame white students. State University of New York at Binghamton offered a program provocatively titled, "#StopWhitePeopl2k16." Pomona College informed its white students that, "You are white, so it is inevitable that you have unconsciously learned racism." Oregon State University held segregated social justice retreats that empowered non-whites. "If in decades ahead, we are as white as we are today," the president of Western Washington University told his students, "we will have failed as a university." California State University students are required to take a diversity course in order to graduate.

Some schools go even further. The paid undergraduate internship program at the University of Minnesota is open only to non-white applicants. "It's shocking that a major university would make educational opportunities open only to students of a certain skin color," said Bill Jacobson, president of the Equal Protection Project. "There is no good form of racial discrimination. Depriving white students of educational opportunities does not promote racial or any other form of justice. The remedy for racism can never be more racism."

And let's not leave out our public educational system. Seattle Public Schools taught its teachers that the education system is guilty of "spirit murder" against black children and that white teachers must "bankrupt their privilege" in acknowledgement of their "thieved inheritance." San Diego Public Schools accused white teachers of being colonizers on stolen Native American land and told them "you are racist" and "you are upholding racist ideas, structures, and policies." Buffalo Public Schools has taught students that all white people perpetuate systemic racism. After being forced to watch a video of dead black children, Buffalo kindergarteners were warned about "racist police and state-sanctioned violence" both of which might kill them at any time.

"Virtually every significant corporation, academic institution, and public employer has these types of training," says Peter Kirsanow of the US Commission on Civil Rights. "This is maybe the most pernicious ideology we've ever seen in the US."

Is it fair to demand that white Americans deconstruct their racism? Are all these anti-white training sessions justified? Consider this answer from Heather Mac Donald in *When Race Trumps Merit: How the Pursuit of Equity Sacrifices Excellence, Destroys Beauty, and Threatens Lives*:

> *"The vast majority of white Americans are decent, well-meaning people who yearn for a post-racial country and don't give a damn about race. White Republicans have had one love affair after another with black politicians and public figures. Some voted for Barack Obama. What matters to those Republicans is not someone's skin color but whether he is perceived as sharing their values."*

You would never realize the truth of Mac Donald's statement if you paid attention to the propaganda being disseminated by anti-racist training. President Trump, through the US Office of Management and Budget, directed a crackdown on anti-racism trainings held for federal employees, referring to the trainings as "divisive, anti-American propaganda." President Biden seems to love them and has reversed Trump's policy.

Indoctrinate Them When They Are Young

Students in schools across the country are being coerced to confess that they are flawed if they happen to be white. The *New York Post* exposed the Bank Street School, an elite private school in Manhattan where they are teaching white students as young as five that "they're born racist and should feel guilty about benefiting from white privilege." White parents have complained about how their children are indoctrinated into thinking that systemic racism still exists, that they are part of the problem, and that "any success they achieve is unearned." Parents are upset that the school "deliberately instills in white children a strong sense of guilt about their race." A six-year-old came home in tears, saying, "I'm a bad person."

Schools everywhere are teaching this defamatory anti-white garbage to students. You wouldn't think the argument could go very far but, thanks to white guilt, it has taken off like a ball of fire. The testimony of Brad Taylor, a student at Rosemont High School in Rosemont, MN, gives a realistic flavor of what white students are going through:

"On the first day of school, our principal gave us a heartfelt speech about equality and standing together. He began to list countless races expressing how much they matter, but never once mentioned [whites]. I don't need you to tell me that I matter but hearing the condolences given to other races and leaving just one race out you inevitably feel you've done something wrong. You must admit how uncomfortable it would be to be characterized just by your skin color on the first day of school. Our principal created unwarranted boundaries and barriers between students, pitting us against each other based on characteristics we can't control. When I questioned why the equity statement couldn't represent all students, they told me that to even ask that question was outlandish and offensive. When I asked them why that was, they told me that 'whites have a pretty good situation right now.' Is that not racism, disregarding my

question merely because of the color of my skin? After a year of the people in charge telling me that I'm a racist and I'm privileged and pointing out our irreversible differences, I've never noticed race more and it's become the first thing I notice when I meet someone—which has never before been the case."

On Your Knees, Whitey!

Whites are being brainwashed to hate themselves and many are capitulating. No one wants to be called "racist." Because of this, gullible whites are surrendering to the demand of Black Lives Matter thugs that whites should genuflect before black people. I didn't believe it until someone showed me a video of a large crowd of whites on their knees in Bethesda, Maryland, as they were led through a mass confession of their alleged racism. It reminded me of the Chinese Cultural Revolution where victims were forced to admit various crimes before a crowd of people who would verbally and physically abuse them.

Under the false flags of "systemic racism" and "white supremacy," the inquisition demands that all white people— no exceptions—confess their racism and take complete responsibility for the problems of the black community. White people must make amends in the form of wealth and power redistribution. David Horowitz, author of *I Can't Breathe: How a Racial Hoax Is Killing America*, is appalled by this blatant assault on the majority of Americans. "The fact that white people are better off is not a privilege," he says.

THE WAR ON WHITES

"It's earned." America runs because of white people and their value system.

Today's big lie, says Colin Flaherty in *Don't Make the Black Kids Angry*, is: "White racism is everywhere. White racism is permanent. White racism explains everything. That is the biggest lie of our generation. Because just the opposite is true. Black crime and violence against whites, gays, women, seniors, young people and lots of others is astronomically out of proportion."

David Horowitz calls the US "the least racist country in history." Somali-born Dutch-American activist Ayaan Hirsi Ali agrees. "What the media do not tell you," she says, "is that America is the best place on the planet to be black, female, gay, trans, or what have you." The existence of pervasive white racism has been denied by many respected black figures. "The oppression of black Americans is over with," black author Shelby Steele explained on Fox News' *Life, Liberty and Levin*. "It is likely," Steele said, "that today's racial disparities are due more to dysfunctions within the black community."

White America has been mostly passive about the blitz of anti-white hate—perhaps because of white guilt, perhaps because of fear of violent reprisals, perhaps because so many people are uninformed. No one wants to be called "racist." At the same time, "more whites have begun talking about themselves as a racially oppressed majority," reports *CNN*. "In a widely publicized survey, white Americans said they suffer from racial discrimination more than blacks."

ED BRODOW

Biden's Federal Government is Anti-White

President Biden's recent executive order on equity (see Chapter Six) gives the green light to extensive government enforcement of the anti-white inquisition. What this means is that Biden is erasing the gains made by the civil rights movement as well as the hope expressed by Dr. King that people will be judged by the content of their character instead of the color of their skin.

Did you hear about it? Probably not, because the mainstream media do not report Biden's anti-white policies. It should have reverberated throughout the media but, with the exception of Fox, there was nothing. Our media don't want the public to be aware of what Biden is doing to encourage divisiveness. "Joe Biden institutes a government-wide system of racial discrimination that dwarfs Jim Crow," Tucker Carlson said on *Fox News*, "and nobody seems to notice."

Tucker Carlson is one of the few to acknowledge that it happened. On his Fox show airing Friday, February 17, 2023, Carlson described Biden's new policy initiative as, "The largest racial tracking bureaucracy since the fall of Nazi Germany. Biden restructured the entire executive branch of the US government to discriminate on the basis of immutable characteristics."

Biden's new order—*Further Advancing Racial Equity and Support for Underserved Communities Through the Federal Government*—requires that within 30 days, every federal agency must have an equity team to coordinate the implementation of Biden's racist initiative. The equity teams will report to an equity czar who will ensure that all new federal employees will be selected based upon their skin color so that preference can be given to non-whites.

"Henceforth," said Tucker Carlson, "every official Joe Biden hires will be a first. Not a first in achievement. The first in appearance. The first person who looks a certain way. Not only can you judge a book by its cover, you are required to." If you are a white male, go hide in the corner. This is now the official policy of the US government.

"Every single person in the US will qualify for one of Joe Biden's many protective categories except straight white men," said Carlson. "They will not be protected because they are, by virtue of being straight and white and male, the cause of the problem. They are the enemy. Don't expect a government contract or an SBA loan or even decent service from the clerk at the DMV. You're a domestic enemy now. You're an English-speaking version of Vladimir Putin. The equity agenda is your personal sanctions regime. Someday we'll wonder how this could have happened in a country that claims to love the civil rights movement."

Equity and Disparate Impact

My generation was taught that we should aim for equality of opportunity. Equal treatment under the law. A colorblind society. Well guess what—things have changed. Now the woke crowd says the hell with equality, what we really need is "equity." The objective of equity is not equality of opportunity, but rather equality of outcome. Everyone should have the same income, job success, house, neighborhood, etc. According to equity and critical race theory, we must give minorities special treatment in order to even up the scales and compensate for past injustices. Biden's executive order aims to do exactly that.

At this point, I should describe the concept known as *disparate impact*. Disparate impact occurs when an action adversely affects one group of people more than another. Blacks make up approximately 12 percent of the national population. If the arrest rate of blacks exceeds 12 percent, or black prison population exceeds 12 percent, blacks are said to be disparately impacted. In those instances, the Left would argue that it is the fault of racist criminal enforcement.

Equity requires equivalent percentages in all cases. The demand for racial proportionality means that the racial composition of every institution must match the general population. "If hiring and promotion criteria mean that a workplace is not proportionately diverse," says Heather Mac Donald, "then those criteria must be abandoned."

Here is an interesting example of the double standard that is applied to racial proportionality: *Liberalsarenuts.com* has bravely exposed the anti-white brainwashing in TV commercials and shows. "For TV," they write, "white men as the majority of Americans have all but disappeared." In a four-month log of TV commercials, "while the African American population in America is only 12% they were in 94.3% of the commercials. Black males are only 5% of our population yet were in 89.7% of the ads. White males who make up the largest segment of our population were in only 4% of the TV commercials! What distorted perception of reality does that serve? They truly do control our entire thought process and will distort our perception of reality, if we allow them to."

If you suggest that racial disparities are caused by differences in achievement or behavioral choices and not by racism, you will be shouted down as a racist—although you are merely alluding to the facts. "The underrepresentation of blacks in many professions," Mac Donald said, "is the result of the unequal distribution of skills, not of bias." For example, American College Testing rated 10 percent of black high school seniors college-ready in math, compared to 44 percent of whites. Only 2 percent of SAT takers with a math score between 750-800 were black. Yet the most desirable jobs in law, finance, medical research, and engineering usually are filled by applicants who fall in the highest range of math scores. If equity is to be the deciding factor in hiring, all of these racial discrepancies must be ignored in favor of hiring unqualified applicants in the name of diversity.

Disparate impact has a negative effect on our culture. "The most devastating charge that can be levelled against a tradition today," says Mac Donald, "is that its practitioners have historically been white. Objectivity, individualism, a respect for the written word, perfectionism, and promptness have been tarred as markers of whiteness because insisting on those values has a disparate impact on blacks. The concept of disparate impact is destroying America's core institutions in the name of fighting invented racism."

To support the equity approach to racial issues, one must accept that the US is inherently racist and that white men have achieved their economic and political objectives by oppressing minorities and women. These ideas have been repudiated by respected black leaders such as Thomas Sowell, Shelby Steele, Bob Woodson, Candace Owens, and Larry Elder. They are unanimous in their agreement that systemic racism and the oppression of blacks are artifacts of the past. "The truth of the matter is," said Shelby Steele, author of *White Guilt: How Blacks and Whites Together Destroyed the Promise of the Civil Rights Era*, "blacks have never been less oppressed than they are today. Opportunity is around every corner. If you are black and you want to be a poet, or a doctor, or a corporate executive, or a movie star, there will surely be barriers to overcome, but white racism will be among the least of them," says Steele. "You will be far more likely to receive racial preferences than to suffer racial discrimination."

"Blacks are now the victims of liberalism and wokeism," said Steele. "That's what's keeping us down, not racism. Past oppression cannot be conflated into present-day oppression. It is likely that today's racial disparities are due more to dysfunctions within the black community." Steele put his finger on the real problem—the black community has become increasingly dysfunctional. A continuing tradition of black violence in urban settings is bringing the civil society to its knees.

"A dysfunctional inner-city culture is hindering black progress," said Heather Mac Donald:

"That culture belittles academic achievement as 'acting white.' It is indifferent to life, as the dozens of drive-by shootings that occur daily in American cities attest to. It is cruel, as shown by the regular beatings and stomping

of elderly Americans, many of them Asian. It is entitled, as the lootings that have become a plague on retail business reveal. America turns its eyes away from this pathological culture and blames itself for phantom racism."

Confessions of a Straight White Male

What was the most significant social development in the US during the twentieth century? Answer: The civil rights movement affirmed the promise of America that race should not determine the destiny of any individual. And the most dramatic change in the last 20 years? The reintroduction of racism with a new twist. We have reverted back to a time when race was responsible for everything by reversing the achievements of Martin Luther King and the movement he personified. Now if you are a straight white male, you are automatically considered a racist, a bigot, and an enemy of the people. Congratulations.

As a heterosexual white male, I was shocked when I discovered that the American Left wants to paint me as an oppressor of my fellow human beings, a modern-day Simon Legree, simply by virtue of my skin color and sexual orientation. Under the false flags of systemic racism and white supremacy, the inquisition demands that all of us white folks confess our racism. Even the president became a promoter of the inquisition when he referred to Kyle Rittenhouse as a white supremacist.

The ideology behind the "all whites are racist" inquisition is called critical race theory. CRT argues that America is inherently racist, that minorities and women are oppressed by whites and especially by white men, and that whites enjoy unearned privileges at the expense of people of color.

According to CRT, if you are white, you are automatically guilty of racism by virtue of your skin color. Two popular books support this abomination (see Chapter Five). *White Fragility* by Robin DiAngelo asserts that if you are white and doubt that you are a racist, it is proof you are a racist. This is classic Catch-22: you're damned if you do and damned if you don't. "A book about racism," says Tucker Carlson, "that is far more aggressively racist than anything Louis Farrakhan has ever written. If you are white, your DNA makes you evil."

The second work is Ibram X. Kendi's anti-white book, *How to Be an Antiracist*. Kendi has openly admitted that he hates white people. "The only remedy to past discrimination," Kendi writes, "is present discrimination." Kendi's thesis is refuted succinctly by black author Shelby Steele. "Past oppression," says Steele, "cannot be conflated into present-day oppression."

Of the top 25 medical schools, 23 are supporting CRT. The AMA has called for identity-based preferences throughout the medical profession. Inequities are blamed on white supremacy, racism, and structural oppression by whites. If you need brain surgery in the days to come, the surgeon may be selected based not on medical school grades but rather on who wins this year's social justice award. Colleges and universities are using a quota system for admission that penalizes white students. President Biden appointed a Supreme Court justice on the basis of her race and sex, not her qualifications. White candidates were excluded from consideration solely because of their race. United Airlines has announced that 50 percent of all new pilots will be chosen from among minorities and women. If white men are more qualified, too bad. From 2024 on, eligibility for winning an Academy Award will be based on race and gender quotas, with an implied emphasis on limiting the participation of whites.

Rather than exhibiting systemic racism, white Americans have bent over backwards to make life better for blacks. "America is not a racist country," agreed Candace Owens. "Anyone claiming otherwise has a vested interest in keeping us divided. The easiest way to maintain power over any group is to keep those within it at war with one another."

An outgrowth of CRT is Black Lives Matter, a Marxist organization that is based on the false narrative that white cops are deliberately killing unarmed blacks. BLM has glorified black violence and placed it on a pedestal. It's not violence, says BLM, it is peaceful protesting for social justice. BLM's destructive influence is growing as the public is manipulated by social media to excuse looting, arson, and murder. It is perpetuated by race baiters such as Jesse Jackson, Al Sharpton, and Oprah Winfrey in order to encourage white guilt and to inflame the black love affair with victimization.

The objective is to foment racial discord. Minority special interest groups are using the banners of equity, diversity, and social justice as a power grab. Supporters of the social justice movement are not seeking justice, they are seeking control. CRT wants to reintroduce racism and segregation to the forefront of American life, and to substitute equity for the equality championed by Dr. King.

Equity means that skin color must determine everything—your job, your promotion, the house you own. The right kind of skin color is black and brown. White is the wrong color. In case you didn't know, that's what your kids are being taught in public schools and elite universities like Harvard, Princeton, and Stanford. That's what Biden's federal government has adopted as its primary domestic strategy.

Many gullible whites are ashamed to be white and apologize every chance they get. They have internalized anti-white arguments and will defend them against people like me, who view them as toxic examples of identity politics. One white woman has received a ton of media coverage because she insists that she is black. Although her white parents dispute this nonsense, she sports an afro, wears a lot of dark makeup, and served as president of the local NAACP chapter.

Giving special treatment to any one group is in violation of the equal protection clause. It is also the worst kind of racism. Blaming current social problems on alleged white oppression heightens racial tensions and keeps the country divided. Are you ready to apologize for your skin color and surrender everything you've worked for to other people based solely on their skin color? You better ... or else the cancel culture will be coming for you.

Teenagers in the black subculture abhor the idea of adopting white values. The worst insult for these kids is to be called "whitey" or "Uncle Tom." This self-destructive behavior—not white privilege—is ruining the lives of millions of African-American kids. Their value system is marked by anger, violence, and refusal to accept personal responsibility. It is reinforced by political correctness, which bashes white people and white values at every opportunity.

Blaming the problems of the black community on white racism is false and misleading, as Shelby Steele has pointed out. "The oppression of black Americans is over with," Steele said. "White institutional racism has disappeared from our society," agrees Scott Greer.

The Self-Hatred of White Americans

The contemporary American Left is a movement predicated on the misguided belief that all traditional American values are insupportable and ought to be replaced. Distilled to its essence, the Left can be identified by a single word: *self-hatred*. For a growing number of Americans, our country sucks. "America has a deep, dark self-destructive secret: We hate ourselves. We hate America," wrote Paul B. Farrell in *MarketWatch*. "A dangerous virus infects America's collective unconscious," he said. "This virus is spreading fast. Americans are consumed with self-hatred."

Farrell describes some of the alleged justifications for our self-hatred: Americans are racist, violent, narcissistic, misogynistic. Americans don't read. They don't work hard anymore. The American Dream is dead. America has alienated the world. Washington is dysfunctional and corrupt. America, says Farrell, has "self-hating superpower disease" and it's crushing our individual and collective souls.

"A new fear stalks white American Democrats," wrote Justin Webb of the BBC at *unherd.com*. "They are horrified by themselves: by the colour of their skin; by the wrongs done by white people and by the system they set up." Scott Greer cites Emory University professor George Yancy, who lays a guilt trip on whites. By virtue of their oppression of people of color, says Yancy, all whites should wage war against themselves.

This self-hatred, said Webb, did not exist 10 years ago. Americans used to be proud of their country and what it stands for. The anti-Vietnam War movement of the 1960s led to a mobilization of leftist sentiment that has coalesced into the cultural insanity we have today.

It took quite a while before we noticed what was going on. The Left's campaign didn't surface until we elected the first black president, a man who hates America and is a child of the leftist movement. From the first day of his presidency, Barack Obama apologized all over the world for what he perceived as America's shortcomings and transgressions. At the core of his message, said *The Heritage Foundation*, was "the concept that the US is a flawed nation that must seek redemption by apologizing for its past 'sins.'"

The destructive forces set loose by Obama are coming to fruition under Biden/Harris. Our rock-solid values—primacy of individual rights over unlimited government power; freedom of speech; the rule of law; meritocracy; equality of opportunity; capitalism; the acceptance of personal responsibility—are under attack as never before. This assault on our values would not be possible without the core belief that we are flawed as a nation and as a people.

This is not to suggest that the US has achieved perfection—far from it—but "never has the core of the country been painted in such a damning light, to be derided so deeply so as to be irredeemable," writes Taylor Lewis at *freethepeople.org.* Elite American institutions have joined the self-hatred bandwagon. Academia, the media, Hollywood, and Big Tech have colluded with the Democratic Party in an all-out assault on American values.

What is the basis of "this America-loathing pathology?" Lewis' answer is that America's elite has "turned against the very country's foundation that provided the means for their prosperity in the first place. The mid-century ideal of America, that of a dynamic nation dedicated to race-less meritocracy, personal liberty, and equality before the law, is outmoded among the modish class. Now it's all white supremacy and systemic oppression all the time, a constant, impenetrable darkness blotting out all light."

The Left's fallacy lies in their intention to throw out the baby with the bathwater. This centuries-old proverb refers to eliminating something good when trying to get rid of something bad. Making an effort to improve the country is "throwing out the bathwater," but completely eradicating American values amounts to "throwing out the baby." To correct perceived abuses, the Left wants the destruction of all existing political, economic, and social institutions as they are creations of a white racist system. While change as a general proposition is desirable and inevitable, it ought not to be accomplished at the expense of everything that is good about the status quo.

Self-hatred has found a similar home in Europe. According to Douglas Murray, author of *The Strange Death of Europe*, cultivated self-distrust and self-hatred have come together to make Europeans unable to argue for their centuries-old culture. He thinks that European civilization as we have known it will not survive. Murray attributes this to two factors. First is the combination of mass Muslim migration into Europe together with low European birth rates. The second is that Europe has "lost faith in its beliefs, traditions, and legitimacy."

In Murray's view, life in Western Europe "has lost its sense of purpose. Whilst incomers will be encouraged to pursue their traditions and lifestyles, Europeans whose families have been here for generations will most likely continue to be told that theirs is an oppressive, outdated tradition, even as they constitute a smaller and smaller minority of the population." It sounds very similar to what is happening on this side of the Atlantic.

Self-hatred can lead to the destruction of America as we know it. "Our economic dynamism and military might can't overcome our own self-doubt, self-hatred, and lack of belief and confidence in America," says Aaron Kliegman. "The manner in which Biden, his team, and their allies in the media have verbally flagellated their country is shameful and detrimental. America must recover its self-belief in order for the 21st century to be another American century and not a Chinese one."

Playing the Race Card

Are you noticing how many items in the news appear to be about anti-black racism? How blacks are an oppressed minority. How police and white supremacists are targeting blacks. How blacks are economically deprived. This was not so before Obama came along. We had the civil rights movement, we had affirmative action, and it seemed like the race issue was evolving smoothly. Systemic racism became a thing of the past.

When people of color say that America is plagued by "systemic racism," says Shelby Steele, what they're really doing is looking for more entitlements. "Blacks have never been less oppressed than they are today," says Steele. "You will be far more likely to receive racial preferences than to suffer racial discrimination." If you believe the media, Steele's assessment can't be true. The liberal media have their own agenda, and it isn't the truth. Whites are bending over backwards to make life better for blacks.

Blacks are being integrated into the American experience. Just watch movies and TV commercials to see the changes that have occurred in American society. Blacks used to complain that they were not adequately represented by Hollywood and Madison Avenue. Today blacks appear in greater numbers than their percentage of the population. If there are two characters in a movie or TV drama, one of them will be black. While this may be a form of social indoctrination, it is a good indication that the country is trying to be responsive to its black population.

Whenever the police are required by circumstances to deal harshly with a black suspect, the race card is automatically dialed up. "Every disparity in arrest or incarceration rates is now attributed to racism," says Heather Mac Donald. Statistics do not support this narrative. Black men commit a disproportionate number of violent crimes. The prevalence of black-on-white crime has been

ED BRODOW

spectacularly ignored by the media. Despite the facts, Black Lives Matter has succeeded in convincing many whites that blacks are being slaughtered by white bigots.

A new attempt to make the national discourse revolve around black people is the 1619 Project. A product of the ultra-liberal *New York Times*, the 1619 Project is an effort to commemorate the 400th anniversary of slavery's beginning in America. It aims to "reframe the country's history, [understand] 1619 as our true founding, and [place] the consequences of slavery and the contributions of black Americans at the very center of the story we tell ourselves about who we are." Sorry liberals, the US is not a white supremacist country and blacks are not the center of the American story.

"Anti-white racism is seeping into history lessons," says Lynn Uzzell in *RealClearPolitics*, "most notably through the curriculum adapted from the *New York Times*' 1619 Project." Nikole Hannah-Jones, who is behind 1619, has alleged that, "The white race is the biggest murderer, rapist, pillager, and thief of the modern world." Hannah-Jones believes that "blackness" is everything that ennobles this country and "whiteness" is everything that debases it. "The 1619 Project has introduced a new form of black supremacy to American history," says Uzzell, "and it has been adopted by over 4,500 schools."

The 1619 Project reinforces identity politics, the aim of which is to divide the country into warring camps based on color and ethnicity. It is all about ancient history. None of it contributes to healing the country in the present moment.

THE WAR ON WHITES

America may not be perfect, but, as David Horowitz affirms in *Big Agenda*, we are "the most tolerant, least racist nation on earth." In *I Can't Breathe*, Horowitz says:

"Racial discrimination, like murder, is illegal, and there are penalties for practicing it. There are thousands of black judges, prosecutors, lawyers, and officers of the law. Where are the legal cases exposing and punishing the implementers of [systemic racism]? There are none, because [racist codes] and systemic racism are political myths invented by the Left to use as weapons against their political opponents."

Donald Trump, who is not given credit for all he did to make lives better for blacks, didn't buy into the racial narrative. Biden is just the opposite. When he blames current social problems on white oppression, it serves to heighten racial tensions. It's time for the media to stop pushing its divisive agenda so the nation can heal itself.

Chapter Two
The Myth of Systemic Racism

An isolated incidence of police brutality in Minneapolis gave the Left an excuse to scream about systemic racism. Many Democratic politicians, under the guise of lamenting George Floyd's demise, are tripping over each other as they get in line to apologize for being white.

"We need systemic change to address the racism in our state and our country," declared Wisconsin Governor Tony Evers. "We must be willing to face it, with clear eyes and open hearts, recognizing that folks who look like me have been part of creating, exacerbating, and benefiting from the systems that we must now turn to dismantle."

Seattle Mayor Jenny Durkan said, "Much of the violence and destruction, both here in Seattle and across the country, has been instigated and perpetuated by white men." These men, who "experience the height of privilege," are taking over "peaceful demonstrations" by people of color, Durkan added.

"The black community is not responsible for what's happening in this country right now," said Governor Gavin Newsom of California. "We are. Our institutions."

Addressing the riots in his state, Governor Andrew Cuomo of New York said, "The real issue is the continuing racism in this country and it is chronic and it is endemic and it is institutional and it speaks to a collective hypocrisy."

The death of George Floyd at the hands of Minneapolis police was a tragedy but it cannot justify either rampant violence or an obscene level of anti-white accusations. The thugs who are looting and burning our cities don't give a hoot about Mr. Floyd. All they care about is taking down the USA. They hope to get away with violence by blaming it on racism. The Floyd incident raises two critical questions: (1) Is America plagued with systemic racism that calls for the dismantling of our social and political institutions? (2) Do racist police and the justice system deliberately discriminate against African-Americans?

Systemic racism no longer exists in the United States. Individual instances of racism are occurring and always will occur—against both blacks and whites—but to suggest that racism is institutionalized ignores the changes that have occurred in the last 60 years. White institutional racism is a thing of the past, said Scott Greer. When people say that America is plagued by systemic racism, says Shelby Steele, "what they're really doing is expanding the territory of 'entitlement." African-Americans are accorded special privileges in every nook and cranny of our society. We elected a black president—twice. What we are experiencing is not systemic racism from whites. It is systemic violence mostly from black people.

"The false charge of systemic racism," said David Horowitz, "is a convenient cover for the Left's inability to identify actual racists directly responsible for inequalities in American life. It is unable to do so because America's culture is so egalitarian and *anti*-racist that the numbers of actual racists (outside the Left itself) are so few, and their impact so inconsequential, that they don't amount to a national problem. Systemic racism is a political myth invented by the Left to advance its destructive agenda."

"America is now the least racist white-majority society in the world," said black Harvard sociologist Orlando Patterson. "[America] has a better record of legal protection of minorities than any other society, white or black; and offers more opportunities to a greater number of black persons than any other society, including all of Africa."

"When I visit university campuses today," says Shelby Steele, "black students often tell me that racism is everywhere around them, that the university is a racist institution. When I ask for specific examples of racist events or acts of discrimination, I invariably get nothing at all or references to some small slight that requires the most labored interpretation to be seen as racist."

David Horowitz and John Perazzo, writing in *FrontPage Magazine*, debunked the systemic racism argument:

"All forms of institutional and systemic racism including Jim Crow were outlawed by the Civil Rights Act of 1964. In one of his first statements as president Biden claimed that 'systemic racism has been built into every aspect of our system.' This is a bald-faced lie. The opposite is the truth. Under the 14th Amendment and the Civil Rights Act of 1964, systemic racism is outlawed in America. With the exception of affirmative action policies sanctioned by the Supreme Court, there is no systemic racism in

THE WAR ON WHITES

America. If there were systemic racism, there would be a tsunami of legal suits to punish those who practiced it. There is no such tsunami because the claim is a baseless lie."

Every other item in the news is about systemic racism and how blacks are oppressed by white people. This towering falsehood is utilized by criminal groups like Black Lives Matter to excuse looting, arson, and murder. Race baiters such as Jesse Jackson, Al Sharpton, and Oprah Winfrey use it to perpetuate the black love affair with victimization. This narrative is completely upside down.

Rather than exhibiting systemic racism, white Americans have tried to make life better for blacks. History bears this out. By giving their lives to end slavery, enabling the civil rights movement, instituting affirmative action, and voting twice for a black president, white America has shown itself to be anything but racist. Based on the historical record, the demand for a blanket apology from whites cannot be justified.

The apology we deserve is from blacks who have poisoned our country with massive crime, violence, chronic anger and hostility, self-victimization, anti-white racism, anti-Semitism, and unwillingness to accept American values of hard work, family, and taking personal responsibility. There are more than a few blacks who expect to achieve the American Dream without having to earn it like everybody else. Instead, they insult whites by calling their extensive achievements "white privilege." If we continue to reward substandard behavior by blacks or anyone else, America—and all the good things we associate with it—will go up in flames. It is time to receive appreciation from blacks for living in the least racist nation on earth.

The systemic racism argument is used by race baiters to avoid a truthful discussion of the damage done to our country from antisocial behavior by non-whites. When whites talk about blacks, they do so with kid gloves, apologetically, carefully so as to avoid giving offense. It has become impossible to say anything critical of blacks without somebody calling you a racist.

Any person attempting to express honest views on the race problem is labeled a racist, if he is white, or an Uncle Tom, if he is black. "We are repeatedly told by liberals—both whites and blacks—that America needs an honest dialogue on race," said Dennis Prager. "Needless to say, they don't mean it, because the moment a white or a black says anything critical of black behavior, he is labeled racist or Uncle Tom. So most non-liberal whites and blacks just keep quiet."

Will the Real Racist Please Stand Up

Most if not all of my white friends are inclined to empathize with African-Americans and how they have been treated in this country. Were it otherwise, Barack Obama would never have been elected to the presidency. At the same time, millions of white Americans are disturbed by their ambivalence toward blacks.

The ambivalence arises when whites are exposed to the angry, violent behavior of large segments of the African-American population as witnessed in crime statistics, rioting, anti-white sentiments often expressed by blacks, and the occasions when angry blacks act out their hostility as they confront whites in public. But because of political correctness, most whites are terrified to admit that they hold critical opinions.

Being racist and having critical opinions are not the same thing. There is not one white person in my acquaintance who harbors a racist attitude towards blacks. Yet most white people I know have admitted to me privately that their personal experiences with black behavior have been overwhelmingly unpleasant. My friends have been on the receiving end of anti-white hate in the form of verbal and physical assaults from black people. When blacks moved in, their neighborhoods deteriorated into a downward spiral of crime, squalor, and decay.

You can't fault people for paying attention to their experience. It is not racism. It is a response to behaviors, not to skin color. Even Jesse Jackson once said, "There is nothing more painful to me than to walk down the street and hear footsteps and start thinking about robbery, then look around and see somebody white and feel relieved."

I was born in a mixed-race neighborhood in Brooklyn, New York. Over a ten-year period, the area became almost exclusively black. The new residents brought crime, violence, and fear. In what has been given the pejorative term, "white flight," most of the white families moved to other city neighborhoods or to the suburbs. Who could blame them? My family stayed put. As more blacks moved in, we had to live with constant stress from exploding black crime and anti-white assaults.

My knowledge of the black community is based on first-hand experience. My neighbors were black. The kids I went to school with were black. The people I rode with on the *A Train* were black, as were the people who shopped in my local market. I did not have to create an imaginary scenario for black America. What I witnessed on a daily basis was a segment of our population that was out of control. Here were people who regularly acted out their anger, who treated each other with contempt, and whose religion was self-pity. The anti-white hostility—no, let's call it racism—from our black neighbors was palpable.

Thanks to black violence, my experience of walking down the street was closer to Beirut than Brooklyn. When you have been mugged and cursed and knocked down because your skin color is white, you are less sympathetic to the "systemic racism" argument.

Systemic Racism or Black Violence?

The idea that people with white skin are inherently flawed is absurd on its face. The value system that has made the US successful as a nation is an achievement of white people. Whites created a society, a work in progress, that is able to correct itself in response to changing times. Like it or not, white people are responsible for the country that people from all over the world want to move to. In contrast, people in the black subculture hold themselves back by deliberately rejecting white values—the rule of law, education, family, the work ethic, meritocracy, taking personal responsibility. This self-destructive behavior—not white racism or white privilege—is ruining the lives of millions of blacks.

The assumption of Black Lives Matter is that blacks can claim a monopoly as objects of bigotry. Try telling that to Hispanics, Jews, Irish, Italians, Asians and other groups that have been on the receiving end of discrimination and intolerance. Watch movies like *Gentlemen's Agreement* and *Gangs of New York* if you want to understand that racism is not aimed solely at blacks. In fact, blacks are considered by many to be more racist than any other group. A Rasmussen poll reported that 37 percent of American adults think most black Americans are racist, while only 15 percent say the same about whites.

It was a big deal in 1947 when Jackie Robinson broke the color line in professional sports. Today, 74 percent of NBA players are black. African-Americans are accorded special privileges—"black privilege"—in every nook and cranny of our country.

"Black Americans now have every opportunity that white Americans have long enjoyed," said Scott Greer. It is not white privilege that prevents blacks from doing better, says author David Horowitz, it is black behavior—the propensity to commit violent crimes, the inability to build intact families, and the unwillingness to accept personal responsibility. Black women do not take responsibility for having children out of wedlock and black fathers do not take responsibility for supporting their children.

The term systemic racism has "no meaning," says black economist Thomas Sowell. "You hear this phrase, 'systemic racism,' 'systemic oppression.' You hear it on our college campuses. You hear it from very wealthy and fabulously famous sports stars. What does that mean?" Sowell asks. "And whatever it means, is it true? It really has no meaning that can be specified and tested in the way that one tests hypotheses. It does remind me of the propaganda tactics of Joseph Goebbels during the age of the Nazis, in which he's supposed to have said that, 'People will believe any lie if it is repeated long enough and loud enough.' It's one of many words that I don't think even the people who use it have any clear idea what they're saying. Their purpose served is to have other people cave in."

Civil rights activist Bob Woodson issued a sweeping indictment of the idea that "systemic racism" is the cause of black hardship in the US. "I don't know what systemic racism is. Maybe someone can explain what that means," Woodson said on *Tucker Carlson Tonight.* "After 50 years of liberal Democrats running the inner cities, where we have all of these inequities, race is being used as a ruse, as a means of deflecting attention away from critical questions such as, why are poor blacks failing in systems run by their own people?"

To be truthful about the causes of social disruption in the US, we must point a finger not at white America but rather at the black community. In spite of a continuing history of violence, blacks are not being held responsible for their behavior. The leftist canard that racist police and the justice system deliberately discriminate against African-Americans is a lie. In 2023, it is ridiculous to suggest that white police are gunning for blacks.

THE WAR ON WHITES

Black men make up six percent of the US population. In 2015, according to Heather Mac Donald in *The War on Cops*, blacks were charged with 62 percent of all robberies, 57 percent of murders, and 45 percent of assaults in the 75 largest US counties. Blacks in New York City committed 75 percent of all shootings, 70 percent of robberies, and 66 percent of all violent crime. One-third of all black males have a felony conviction. Ignoring the obvious connection between black criminality and black incarceration, the Left continues to blame the police. The bulk of responsibility, said former New York Mayor Rudy Giuliani, is on blacks who "commit murder eight times more per capita than any other group in our society."

"The fault lies primarily with the black criminals," says political commentator Dennis Prager, "not with a racist society." Black talk show host Larry Elder agrees. "Numerical disparities result from differences of offending," he said, "not because of racism."

"If there is a bias in police shootings after crime rates are taken into account," said Mac Donald, "it is against white civilians."

Holding Blacks Responsible for Their Choices

Blacks lag behind other groups in economic success, safe neighborhoods, and family cohesiveness. The question is, who or what is responsible? Heather Mac Donald contends that blacks must be held responsible for their own negative behaviors. The notion that blacks are victims of a racist society may have been true prior to the 1960s, she says, but this is a half-century after the civil rights movement.

"When Americans are viewed as individuals responsible for their decisions," says David Horowitz, "it is apparent that disparities in income, education, and even susceptibility to diseases flow principally from poor choices made by individuals who fail to take advantage of the opportunities available to them in a country where discrimination by race or gender is illegal."

Poor individual choices made by blacks have been reinforced by government interference in the form of entitlements. Encouraging blacks not to take responsibility for their own lives has been part of the Democratic Party's plan to make them dependent on government handouts. The black family, claims *The Heritage Foundation*, was destroyed by "the progressive term 'compassion' during the War on Poverty, which began in 1964." The number of African-American lives damaged or destroyed by Democratic Party welfare policies, says David Horowitz, "would exceed the wildest dreams of any klansman."

"Centuries of slavery, generations of Jim Crow did not destroy the black family," said Thomas Sowell. "But one generation of the welfare state did." The legacy of the Left's welfare system is the break-up of low-income black families, the explosion of out-of-wedlock births, systemic poverty, higher black crime statistics and rates of incarceration, and the substantial decrease of black households headed by someone who works.

The primary fallacy of the Left's redistribution plan is that it does nothing to end the pattern of black poverty. The current system of welfare entitlements benefits no one other than the charter members of the Victimization Industry, people like Jesse Jackson and "Rev." Al Sharpton. Entitlements foster a victim mentality that places the blame on whites. "Victimhood has become a mental plague on black America," says black activist Candace Owens.

The rationale for the welfare state is the perception that low-income blacks can't make it on their own. "The problem is that Washington is building a culture of dependency," reports *CNN*, "with ever more people relying on an ever-growing federal government to give them cash or benefits." No group has been impacted by this more than blacks. Under this culture of dependency, black welfare recipients lose the work habits and job skills that would otherwise make them independent.

By providing a steady stream of income to unwed black mothers, the welfare system has eliminated black fathers because payments are tied to their absence. *The Heritage Foundation* has called out black men for "the largest-scale abandonment of women by men in human history." Poverty is being transferred from generation to generation with no hope in sight. "You cannot take any people, of any color," said Thomas Sowell, "and exempt them from the requirements of civilization—including work, behavioral standards, personal responsibility and all the other basic things that the clever intelligentsia disdain—without ruinous consequences to them and to society at large."

ED BRODOW

White Privilege and Other Lies
About Race in America

The progressive liberal playbook includes a handful of concepts that are designed to enhance what I call the "tyranny of the minority"—the power of special interest groups achieved at the expense of the white majority. In addition to *social justice, diversity, multiculturalism,* and *toxic masculinity,* one of the most effective schemes invented by the Left is known as *white privilege*—"a weapon," said David Horowitz in *The Enemy Within,* "designed to cripple and destroy white people."

White privilege points to the unfairness of societal advantages that allegedly benefit all people identified as white. "Racial privilege is exclusive to whites as a group," says Scott Greer, "and is completely unearned, according to those who buy into the concept. Whites should not be so quick to tout their achievements when they are ill gotten, according to white privilege theory. White privilege is essentially a concept for explaining how a nation that no longer tolerates institutional racism still discriminates against nonwhites." The Left wants white people to confess and atone for those advantages. It has been argued that white privilege, when abused, can lead to horrible crimes committed against society. Despite the rhetoric, the white privilege argument is nothing more than a racist attack on Caucasians.

As a young man, the only "white privilege" I enjoyed was the knowledge that the American Dream was within reach if I earned it. In school, the military, and the world of work, whatever success I achieved was based on my striving for excellence. I studied with diligence, cleaned toilets at night to pay for a college education, met the exacting standards of Marine Corps Officer Candidates School, and always went the extra mile to be the best at my profession. To hell with all that, says the white privilege crowd. Whatever success I have achieved is because of an unjust system that favors white people.

The president is not helping the situation. "Biden has cited white supremacist domestic terrorists as the biggest threat to the nation so often that many Americans now believe him," wrote Kathleen Brush in *American Thinker*. Brush cites Attorney General Garland's speech on June 15, 2021, in which he said, "In the FBI's view, the top domestic violent extremist threat comes from racially or ethically motivated violent extremists, specifically those who advocate for the superiority of the white race."

The question is, who or what is responsible for minority problems? The Left insists that the blame belongs squarely on the shoulders of white people. That is the argument of DiAngelo's *White Privilege*. Not so, says David Horowitz, it is African-American behavior. Many teenagers in the black subculture hold themselves back by deliberately rejecting mainstream values. This self-destructive behavior—not white privilege—is responsible for racial disparities.

Political commentator Bill O'Reilly believes that the white privilege argument encourages blacks not to take personal responsibility. When you realize that this negative value is already a cancer in black America, blaming white people only compounds an existing problem. *Wall Street Journal* editorial board member Jason Riley, who is black, has accused civil rights leaders of being more interested in "blaming the problems of blacks on white racism" than getting to the real causes. Even white Americans are falling for the white privilege scam, says O'Reilly. They are "making excuses for bad behavior," he says, and "enabling the chaos" in places like Chicago.

Because they depend on the black vote, the Democrats won't do anything—such as telling the truth—that might offend the African-American community. The myth of white privilege is being used to brainwash a generation of Americans. Instead of unfairly shaming white students, what is really needed are indoctrination courses to help minority students take personal responsibility. In blaming white people for all the ills of society, the values of our educational system are upside-down.

"If you are told to talk about white privilege and you said, 'I'm not doing that, I don't have privilege,' you'd be in serious trouble," wrote Douglas Murray in *The War on the West*. "There was a partner in KPMG who lost his job just because he said he thought implicit bias training was crap. And he was a partner."

Murray cites philosopher Friedrich Nietzsche: "'There is a type of person who tears at wounds long closed and then shrieks about the pain they feel.' We are dealing with a lot of those people at the moment," Murray explains. "They have decided to rip at a long-closed wound and then cry in order to win something, whether pity or money or reparations."

Murray argues that we should not be held responsible for the baggage of the past. "Only one group of people—white westerners—are expected to be responsible for everything that anyone who looked remotely like them in the past did, and everyone else is not."

For the Left, excellence developed by white people in any and all forms of human endeavor should be considered manifestations of systemic racism. The expectation of safe air travel will become a thing of the past as the requirement for competent pilots is discarded as another symptom of white supremacy. No longer will we admire successful businessmen such as the founders of Microsoft, Apple, and Google. Brilliant legal scholars—as functionaries of the white legal system—will be despised. And, of course, the entire structure of American government, including separation of powers and checks and balances, will have to be jettisoned because it was developed by racist white people.

The notion of white privilege ought to be an insult to the intelligence of every American. It is a fantasy concocted so white Americans can be demonized and black Americans can avoid dealing truthfully with their issues. For the sake of our children, we must come to our senses before we wind up with a generation of racially confused neurotics.

Acknowledgment of Black-On-White Crime Is Long Overdue

The unfortunate implication of the George Floyd incident is that blacks are overwhelmingly victimized by whites and, especially, by white police. This is an inversion of reality. The vast majority of racially motivated crimes are committed by blacks against whites. As black educator John McWhorter said, "People walking down the street and getting beaten up by white racist thugs is something quite rare in America."

The prevalence of black-on-white crime, spectacularly ignored by the media, has been chronicled by Colin Flaherty in *Don't Make the Black Kids Angry.* "A new generation of black leaders and white enablers want to remove black violence from the table," Flaherty says. "Black crime and violence against whites, gays, women, seniors, young people and lots of others is astronomically out of proportion."

"Episodes of unprovoked violence by young black gangs against white people chosen at random on beaches, in shopping malls, or in other public places," said Thomas Sowell, "have occurred in Philadelphia, New York, Denver, Chicago, Cleveland, Washington, Los Angeles, and other places across the country. Both the authorities and the media tend to try to sweep these episodes under the rug."

Heather Mac Donald, writing in *City Journal*, agrees. "Whites are the overwhelming target of interracial violence," she says. "Between 2012 and 2015, blacks committed 85.5 percent of all black-white interracial violent victimizations. That works out to 540,360 felonious assaults on whites." Black-on-black crime is even worse, as proven by the daily murder statistics emanating from cities like Chicago, Baltimore, and New York.

All too often, black criminals are supported by local law enforcement. This trend has become a serious problem as Soros-backed prosecutors like Alvin Bragg in New York release felons out onto the streets. City governments around the country are rolling back criminal penalties and enforcement in a futile attempt to eliminate disparities in minority arrests. "If, as anti-racism orthodoxy indicates, the real root causes of higher black crime may not be discussed," says Heather Mac Donald, "then the only way to reduce racial disparities in the criminal justice system is to stop penalizing criminal behavior. The lessons of two decades of successful crime-fighting have been forgotten, with predictable results: spreading violence and predation." If you try to bring attention to this perversion of the justice system, you are automatically called out as racist. The result is that everyone—black and white—is afraid to deal with it.

Matthew Boose, writing in *American Greatness*, had this astute observation:

"[The Left] will always find a way to justify the criminals and blame the real victims, whose cries for justice are drowned out by the endless wailing of black entitlement. We are often told that the politics of 'white grievance' is transforming America into some kind of authoritarian state, but the opposite is true. We are racing into the ghetto."

An example of how the legal system supports black criminality occurred in St. Louis where a white couple, Mark and Patricia McCloskey, attempted to defend their home against a Black Lives Matter mob that trespassed on private property and threatened to kill the white family as they were eating dinner. A video taken by one of the mobsters made it patently clear that this was a case of self-defense. The St. Louis prosecutor apparently did not see the video. In a travesty of justice, she brought assault charges against the white couple. None were brought against the mob.

An even better example took place in Orion Township, Michigan. A white couple was charged with assaulting a black woman and her 15-year-old daughter. According to Takelia Hill, who is black, her 15-year-old daughter Makayla Green was "bumped" by Jillian Wuestenberg, a pregnant white woman, at the entrance to a Chipotle restaurant. Green demanded an apology. Wuestenberg refused. Hill and Green then played the race card, falsely accusing Wuestenberg of racism.

As in the St. Louis case, the incident was filmed— presumably by Green. I watched the video. It is without doubt exhibit A in support of the white couple. As the video begins, the black women are screaming obscenities at Mrs. Wuestenberg, who tries to remain calm. Hill demands an apology as she blocks Wuestenberg from getting into her car. Wuestenberg replies that she did nothing that she need apologize for, then politely asks Hill to get out of her way.

When Mr. Wuestenberg helps his wife get into the front passenger seat, Hill screams at Mrs. Wuestenberg, "You're a white ass bitch." Then Hill turns on Mr. Wuestenberg, screaming, "You say somethin' I'll beat your white ass too." Then she challenges him. "Please do something. Do something. Please put your mother-fucking hands on me." He responds with, "Who do you think you guys are? She did nothing to you." The black women continue to scream and gesticulate. "You're very racist and ignorant," they tell him as he ignores them, turns away, and gets into the driver's side. At no time does he threaten the black women. The white couple weren't arguing back at all, except to deny they were racists and that anything happened.

Hill continues screaming, calling the white woman a racist. "This is not that type of world," Mrs. Wuestenberg replies. "White people are not racist. I care about you and I'm sorry if you had an incident that has made you feel like that." Then she closes the window. At this point, Hill gets behind the car, blocking its exit, and begins pounding on the trunk. The Wuestenbergs get out of the car to defend their property. Hill tries to grab Mrs. Wuestenberg, who pulls a handgun and points it at Hill in an attempt to defend herself from Hill's assault. "Get away," she screams at Hill. When Hill retreats, Wuestenberg puts the gun down, gets in the car, and they pull away.

The white couple were minding their own business when they were threatened and assaulted by two angry black women. There is no doubt this was a case of black-on-white violence. Yet Oakland County Prosecutor Jessica Cooper charged the Wuestenbergs with one count of felonious assault each, a four-year felony. Neither Hill nor Green were charged. In view of the facts, it appears that the prosecutor was seduced by the Black Lives Matter playbook. The presumption was that the white couple was guilty by virtue of their skin color and nothing else. Adding insult to injury, Mr. Wuestenberg was fired from his job at Oakland University, which convicted him in a disgraceful piece of virtue signaling: "We have seen the video and we deem his behavior unacceptable." What did he do that was unacceptable? I thought he kept his cool. The facts in the case were ignored.

Happily, both prosecutions were dismissed, but only after the white participants were forced to endure a great deal of disruption in their lives. When innocent white people like the Wuestenbergs are assaulted by blacks, the legal system bends over backwards to coddle the black perpetrators.

Oh No—It's Karen!

Another example of the support given to blacks at the expense of white people is referring to a white woman as "Karen." *Dictionary.com* defines Karen as "a pejorative slang term for an obnoxious, angry, entitled, and often racist middle-aged white woman who uses her privilege to get her way or police other people's behaviors." This is clearly a racist term that some have called the N word for white women. If there were a comparable term for black women, rioting would follow. But when applied to whites, it is perfectly acceptable. "In America," said Ben Shapiro, "we are allowed to have racial terms for white women."

When there is a confrontation between a white person and a black person, Shapiro said, the Left decrees that the white person must be at fault. "If you are a white person," he said, "you have an obligation to be victimized." Shapiro alluded to the case of Jordan Neely, a violent black man who threatened people on the New York City subway and was subdued by a white former Marine. Although he was acting in self-defense, the Marine was charged with manslaughter. By virtue of his race, said Shapiro, "Neely apparently had a right to threaten people on the subway. These are the dual moralities of the Democratic Party."

THE WAR ON WHITES

"In today's America," said *Fox News* presenter Will Cain, "you are required to take the side of any black person in incidences that also involve a white person. Evidence does not matter. And not only do you have to side with the person of color, you must immediately believe that the incident is racial in nature."

Cain's comment came as he was discussing the controversy over Sarah Comrie, a pregnant physician's assistant in Manhattan, who was falsely accused of taking a rental bike—which she had already paid for—from a group of young black men who attempted to intimidate her. "Sarah Comrie is white, and the five teenagers are black," said Cain, "and therefore, Sarah Comrie is automatically racist and at fault. Those are the rules in America. The media headlines immediately followed those rules, referring to Comrie as a 'Karen', which is a new racial slur for white women." Based on the slanted media coverage, Comrie was suspended from her job at Bellevue Hospital.

"As one of 1.1 million women in the United States named Karen," Karen Kirk wrote in *The Columbus Dispatch*, "seeing my name used as a randomly selected, lazy label for racist, privileged white women behaving badly is soul-crushing." Too bad, Ms. Kirk, that is the price you have to pay for being white.

Calling Someone Racist Without Proof

My 87-year-old buddy plays handball twice a week with three other octogenarians. Their YMCA has two handball courts, one of which is preferred because the lighting is better. One day the senior athletes arrived at the Y only to discover four black women doing their stretching workout on the good handball court. The men, all of whom are white, politely asked the women if they wouldn't mind doing their exercises on the other court so the men could play ball on the court with decent lighting. The women said okay and moved to the other court.

Five minutes later, a member of the YMCA staff informed the handball players that they would have to relinquish their court to the women. Then the staff member lowered the boom. The women claimed the men had used the N word. *Horror of horrors! Send in the Marines.*

The men categorically denied the charge. It didn't matter. The staff member refused to accept the men's denial. The mere accusation by four lying women was sufficient to establish that the dreaded N word had been used. The women were not challenged because convicting a white person of racism without proof is part of the liberal playbook. Welcome to the Left's new rule for establishing culpability: A mere allegation of wrongdoing is sufficient to convict. Say goodbye to the bulwark of our legal system. If you are white, you are guilty until proven innocent.

The same rule—the poison of unsubstantiated allegations—was invoked in another racially charged situation. President Trump was accused by Democratic Sen. Dick Durbin of suggesting that the US should stop accepting immigrants from "shithole countries." Trump is alleged to have said, "Why are we having all these people from shithole countries come here?" According to Durbin, Trump advocated that the US should be taking more immigrants from "countries such as Norway" instead of "shithole" countries like Haiti, El Salvador, and several nations in Africa. His comments allegedly occurred off the record in a meeting between the president and a group of senators. Sen. Durbin called the comments "hate filled, vile, and racist." Durbin, by the way, has a history of making up statements from private White House meetings.

The president issued a denial. "This was not the language used," Trump tweeted. Sens. David Perdue and Tom Cotton, who attended the meeting, backed up Trump's denial by issuing this statement: "In regards to Senator Durbin's accusation, we do not recall the president saying these comments." Despite the president's denial and the concurrence of two senators, the accusation was enough to establish guilt. The mainstream media went absolutely bat crazy with an avalanche of stories accusing Trump of racism because of his "highly incendiary comments."

CNN mouthpieces Anderson Cooper, Don Lemon, Jim Acosta, and Jeffrey Toobin agreed that the alleged outburst proved Trump is a racist. Cooper said on his evening program that the president "is tired of so many black people coming into this country." Trump "seems to harbor racist feelings about people of color, from other parts of the world," said Acosta. "It just shows that, you know, the president has racist views," Toobin said. "I mean, you know, how long do we have to dance around that issue?"

How long do we have to dance around the fake media? The multitude of attacks on the president emanated from an unsubstantiated claim from a single dubious source. Even former Democratic President Jimmy Carter expressed his disgust with the media's eagerness to accept unproven allegations of racism.

Another accusation of racism was from an angry black woman who said TV talk star Bill O'Reilly called her "hot chocolate." This presumably was a reference to her race. As in the case of the octogenarian handball players, introducing the race card only makes O'Reilly look worse in the eyes of a public that has been trained to respond emotionally to specific cues relating to "social justice." Should a respected man's career be destroyed because he called a woman "hot chocolate?" It really seems ridiculous and yet we have reached a place in our social history where racial witch hunts are a regular feature and public figures can be brought down by accusations of racism.

As explained by Colin Flaherty in *Don't Make the Black Kids Angry*, racism is the current excuse being offered by the Democratic Party for the problems afflicting black America. Democrat politicians and their media allies are having a field day with stories about the consequences of alleged white racism. One of the local newspapers in my community called out racism as the cause of all the problems we face. "Racism," the newspaper informed us, "creates disparate outcomes in housing, education, employment, public safety and criminal justice, and health." The Achilles Heel of their argument is revealed by a statement that was slipped in at the end of the article where no one was supposed to see it: "The [county supervisors] blame only racism—*and not any other social factors*—for the disparities." Racism. Racism. Racism. Everything is blamed on racism. White racism, that is.

THE WAR ON WHITES

President Trump attempted to focus attention on the plight of our inner cities. When he used Baltimore as a glaring example ("Baltimore is a living hell"), Trump was accused of racism. Trump criticized black Rep. Elijah Cummings while casting the Baltimore-area district he represents as "dangerous" and "filthy." Sen. Elizabeth Warren, in a vain attempt at virtue signaling, led the charge from the Left. "Elijah Cummings fights for what is just in this country," she said. "To be attacked by a president issuing racist tweets is beyond insulting, it is disgusting. Donald Trump is a racist who makes ever more outrageous, racist remarks," Warren continued. "We need to call out white supremacy for what it is—domestic terrorism."

Bob Woodson, an African-American who founded the Woodson Institute in 1981 to help residents of low-income neighborhoods address the problems of their communities, disagreed with Warren's assessment. In an interview on *Tucker Carlson Tonight*, Woodson eloquently described the problem. Here is what he said:

"As a veteran of the civil rights movement, I find [Warren's] comments insulting, condescending, and patronizing. It also acts as a barrier for the exploration of real solutions that exist for places like Baltimore and low-income blacks. The biggest problem in black America today isn't between whites and blacks—it's internal. Elizabeth Warren and people who continue to emphasize the external enemy are preaching a false solution. Black America's destiny has never been

determined by what white people do or do not do. It deflects attention away from the real problems."

Fortunately, the R word no longer holds the kind of opprobrium that it did in the 1960s. The accusation of racism has been tossed around so carelessly that it no longer packs a punch. "Yesterday's race-baiters were brutal white bullies," says Ben Shapiro. "Today's are left-wingers invoking fictional white racism to achieve their goals."

If racism is not the answer, where does the solution lie? Woodson hit the nail on the head:

"The urban communities where you have the highest crime, the most drug-infested, have been run by liberal Democrats for the last 50 years. The real problem is the kind of betrayal by the leaders of these cities. They can avoid confronting those issues because they use race as a shield. White people could all go to Europe tomorrow and the conditions of the inner cities would not change. If racism were the pervasive problem then why are all blacks not suffering equally? There are three zip codes in Prince Georges County where the median income for black families is $170,000. They are three times richer than most whites."

The signal accomplishment of the civil rights movement was the manifestation of Dr. King's vision of a society where people are judged by the content of their character rather than the color of their skin. People gave their lives to make this happen. Sadly, the Left's campaign for diversity is destroying everything that was accomplished on the streets of Selma. When the Left advocates diversity, they want people to be judged by their skin color. Character becomes irrelevant as the Left divides Americans into competing groups based on color and ethnicity. Out of this perversion of Dr. King's dream, we are plagued with arbitrary accusations of racism.

President Trump was not a racist for trying to solve the problems of our decaying cities. He was doing his job. "It's time to stop this preoccupation with race," said Bob Woodson, "and come together to address the problems of low-income people of all races because answers exist. We can't do it as long as we stay stuck on the race grievance issue."

Accusations that Donald Trump is a Racist

For the past seven years, Democrats have fielded a vicious campaign to discredit Donald Trump. This campaign has the support of most of the people who work in government jobs—the Deep State—as well as more than a few Republicans. As a beltway outsider, Trump's intention to drain the Washington "swamp" threatens all of these people. Trump Derangement Syndrome is a name that has been given to the rabid attacks on the former president. One of the avenues employed by Trump-haters is the allegation that Trump is a racist. The media has run with this.

Nothing could be further from the truth. Trump's history as a businessman includes support for civil rights causes together with the promotion of women and minorities to jobs in the Trump organization. Accusations of anti-Semitism are patently ridiculous when you realize that Trump's daughter and grandchildren are Jewish. None of that matters to Trump-haters.

As an alpha male Republican, Trump is the perfect target for an anti-white onslaught.

The Trump-hating *New York Times* has led the charge. The leaking of a secret recording exposed the *Times'* intention to push the "Trump is a racist" angle. Dean Baquet—the first black American to serve as the *Times'* executive editor—told his staff that, in light of the failure of the "Trump and the Russians" campaign, they should focus on Trump's alleged racism. The *Times* will do anything to "get Trump."

"The Failing New York Times," Trump tweeted in response to the leak, "in one of the most devastating portrayals of bad journalism in history, got caught by a leaker that they are shifting from their Phony Russian Collusion Narrative to a Racism Witch Hunt. Journalism has reached a new low in the history of our Country. It is nothing more than an evil propaganda machine for the Democrat Party. The reporting is so false, biased and evil that it has now become a very sick joke."

Ibram X. Kendi is typical of those who accuse Trump of racism. On page 8 of Kendi's racist tome, *How to Be an Antiracist*, the author devotes a section to his attack on Trump. One accusation is that Trump's push for a border wall is racist. In fact, Trump's objection to an open border has nothing to do with race, but is a response to concerns about drugs, disease, Mexican cartels, border integrity, and the lack of infrastructure to accommodate millions of illegals.

THE WAR ON WHITES

Kendi also repeats an oft-cited criticism that Trump allegedly made racist comments following a 2017 white supremacist rally in Charlottesville, Virginia. Trump's statement was seen by critics as implying moral equivalence between the white supremacist marchers and those who protested against them. Kendi claims that Trump praised the white supremacists as being "very fine people." What Trump actually said was that not counting the violent protesters, there also were fine people on both sides. Trump later said, "I'm not talking about the neo-Nazis and the white nationalists, because they should be condemned totally." The media and Kendi have completely misrepresented his remarks.

In another case of misrepresentation by the media, Trump was accused of calling all immigrants "criminals and rapists." This one also got under Kendi's skin. Trump actually was referring to criminals and not to the general Hispanic population. "I'm referring, and you know I'm referring, to the MS-13 gangs that are coming in," Trump explained. "When MS-13 comes in, when the other gang members come into our country, I refer to them as animals. And guess what—I always will."

Trump has been criticized for a 1989 interview with Bryant Gumbel, where Trump stated, "A well-educated black has a tremendous advantage over a well-educated white in terms of the job market." Not only is that not racist, it shows foresight into the current job market in which, as I explain in Chapter Three, employers are jumping up and down for a chance to hire minority applicants.

ED BRODOW

Trump was also accused of racism when he called Baltimore "a living hell," describing some areas of the city as "dangerous" and "filthy." Sen. Elizabeth Warren responded by saying, "Donald Trump is a racist who makes ever more outrageous, racist remarks." Never mind that what Trump said was absolutely true.

Trump is demonstrably not a racist. The numerous attempts to prove that he is are examples of targeted racism against a straight white alpha male.

Only White People Can Be Racist

Bashing white people is acceptable to the Left, says Ben Shapiro, because they believe that racism can only come from dominant groups. Only whites can be bigots. Non-white people cannot be racist. This is the lame argument made by Robin DiAngelo in *White Fragility*. When Sarah Jeong of the *New York Times* attacks white people, the Left claims it is not actually racism.

The basis for this self-serving argument was articulated by Scott Greer. Under the new racial hierarchy, he says, "nonwhites cannot be racists due to historically controlled power in Western societies." Only the powerful can be racist. *White Fragility* and other racist books offer the same specious reasoning.

Symone Sanders, a "woman of color" and adviser to both Bernie Sanders and Joe Biden, has claimed that "*we don't need white people leading the Democratic party.*" She is not accused of racism because the Left believes that only minorities can be the object of racism.

THE WAR ON WHITES

Is there such a thing as anti-white racism? *Wikipedia* has this to say: "Allegations of reverse racism emerged prominently in the 1970s, building on the racially color-blind view that any preferential treatment linked to membership in a racial group was morally wrong." Ben Shapiro agrees. "I'm all for one standard when it comes to racism," Shapiro says. "Don't malign racial groups. Don't treat one racial group differently than you would treat another racial group. The Left is totally okay with racism as long as it's against white people. There is a massive double standard in the US. Racism is okay so long as it is being performed by people who are not white against people who are white."

Whites are not the only group capable of racist behavior. White people don't hold a monopoly when it comes to bigotry. A Rasmussen poll reported that 37% of American adults think most black Americans are racist, while only 15% say the same about whites. "When, when, when," Larry Elder asked, "will [Obama] say something, anything about the cancer of anti-white black racism?"

"A majority of whites say discrimination against them exists in America today," reports NPR, "according to a poll released from NPR, the Robert Wood Johnson Foundation, and the Harvard T.H. Chan School of Public Health. *Wikipedia* claims that whites tend to think anti-black racism has largely disappeared, "to the point that they see prejudice against white people as being more prevalent." More than half of whites—55 percent—surveyed say that, generally speaking, they believe there is discrimination against white people in America today. A majority (57%) of white respondents to a 2016 survey by the Public Religion Research Institute said they believed discrimination against white people was as significant a problem as discrimination against black people. Researchers at Tufts University and Harvard report that as of the early 2010s many white Americans feel as though they suffer the greatest discrimination among racial groups.

The status of anti-white hate was summed up by Lynn Uzzell in *RealClearPolitics*:

> *"Anti-white racism is today a greater problem, at least in the white-collar world, than anti-black racism. For anyone who may be skeptical that anti-white racism is now worse than anti-black racism, consider this: Overt acts of anti-black discrimination today are socially, politically, and professionally unimaginable. Anti-white discrimination, on the other hand, has become almost an institutional requirement. Schools and businesses seem fearful lest they are accused of not doing enough to stereotype, denigrate, marginalize, and suppress 'whiteness.'"*

There is a double standard when it comes to commenting on racism. Proof of this was supplied when cartoonist Scott Adams accused blacks of being a hate group. Citing statistics that most blacks don't like whites, Adams said that whites should stay away from blacks altogether. The media went into a frenzy, removing Adams' popular cartoons from their newspapers. The hypocrisy was pointed out by Ben Shapiro. "If that were reversed," he said, "the entire media would be putting this guy on the front page, he is now speaking on major college campuses, he would be given op-ed spaces over at the New York Times." In fact, that is exactly what happened when Robin DiAngelo suggested that whites are a hate group (see Chapter Five).

It's Time to Delegitimize Racial Tantrums

Glorification by the media of Black Lives Matter—a criminal, Marxist organization—has given a small but vocal cadre of mentally unbalanced individuals in the black community the license to cry "white supremacy" and "systemic racism" every time they feel the need to experience a tantrum. Expressing support for blacks should not require the vilification of whites, yet that is exactly what we are witnessing with black behavioral tantrums.

Before BLM, overt anti-white language and behavior were unacceptable. Now anything that is arguably a product of white people—the American Dream, economic success, the rule of law, medical advances, Western civilization—is a legitimate target of black anger. The crudest example of black tantrum is the epidemic of riots, looting, and arson that has become commonplace since the George Floyd incident.

The irony is that the legitimization of racial tantrums is harmful to "people of color." Giving in to extremist race-based demands will only make life worse for blacks. Tolerating racial tantrums means we accept that blacks are inferior and so they should not be held accountable if they exhibit inferior behavior. George W. Bush referred to this as "the soft bigotry of low expectations." It is the basis for the Democratic Party's welfare state.

The message we have been sending to African-Americans is: "You are not smart enough or capable enough to compete, so we will give you welfare payments, food stamps, Medicaid, free cellphones, and affirmative action." The low expectations implicit in the welfare system have resulted in tragic consequences for the black community.

A more sophisticated version of the black tantrum is the *New York Times* initiative known as the 1619 Project. This attempt to revise American history argues that "white racist supremacy is irrevocably intertwined in the country's DNA," says black entrepreneur Ian Rowe. The 1619 Project unwittingly supports the notion of black victimization. "It grants to the white race a wicked superiority, treating them as an oppressive people too powerful for black Americans to overcome," says black Congressman Burgess Owens. "It brands blacks as hapless victims devoid of the ability, which every other culture possesses, to assimilate and progress."

Blacks must be encouraged to believe that they possess the ability to meet "white" standards. The alternative, lowering standards across the board in order to make it easier for blacks, will negatively impact everyone. At a time when we are in a race with China, every effort must be made to defend American standards of excellence. We can't do that as long as we legitimize racial tantrums.

The *Times* Wants to Drive Identity Politics Down Your Throat

The "1619 Project" developed by the *New York Times* is propaganda pandering to the new liberal playbook. Slavery

THE WAR ON WHITES

was never the central issue in the founding and development of the United States. The experience of slavery was a major factor but not the defining one by any means.

The left-wing *Times* has pushed the false argument that the US is characterized by systemic racism coming from a majority composed of white supremacists. The US is not a white supremacist country and blacks are not the center of the American story. Blacks did not found the US—Britain gets the credit for that, as well as the credit for introducing slavery to North America. Slavery was never the focus of US population centers. And what about the prevalence of indentured servitude among the white settlers? Make no mistake about it, the 1619 Project is an attempt to re-write history as the *Times* kisses the butts of liberals who hate America. It reinforces identity politics, the aim of which is to divide the country into warring camps based on color and ethnicity.

"The whole project is a lie," said former House Speaker Newt Gingrich. "Certainly if you're an African-American, slavery is at the center of what you see as the American experience. But for most Americans, most of the time, there were a lot of other things going on." Gingrich tweeted that the *Times* should make its slogan, "All the Propaganda we want to brainwash you with." Gingrich's conclusion: "The *New York Times*' editor, he basically said, look, we blew it on Russian collusion, didn't work. Now we're going to go to racism, that's our new model. The next two years will be Trump and racism. This is a tragic decline of the *New York Times* into a propaganda paper worthy of *Pravda* or *Izvestia* in the Soviet Union."

Echoing Gingrich's point-of-view, conservative commentator Eric Erickson wrote on his blog: "The inmates have taken over the asylum and those inmates are re-writing American history to make everything about race, racism, and slavery." Dean Baquet, the *Times*'s executive editor, claimed that race "is going to be a huge part of the American story" and that the 1619 Project will "teach readers to think a little bit more like that."

American Spectator, a conservative website, was quick to respond:

> *"It's hard to imagine America's former leading newspaper recovering from what its executive editor admitted last week. Baquet says he 'built our newsroom' to cover a story which turns out to have been based on a hoax spread by Democrat Party operatives and used by a corrupt Obama administration to spy on innocent American citizens while attempting to prejudice a presidential election. Baquet now wants to spend the next two years forcing the ashes of that credibility down the collective throat of the American people by spreading non-stop the further hoax of the president's racism."*

As a divisive tool, the 1619 Project is right up there with political correctness and the Green New Deal. If the *Times* gets away with this fiction, what if the next liberal wave is an argument that Latinos are the "very center" of the American story? After all, the Latino population now exceeds that of African-Americans. Or will the next version of our history place Native Americans at the center? I can see the *Times* headline: "America's original sin was the genocide of Native Americans."

"If the ownership of the *Times* had any integrity or business sense," *American Spectator* concluded, "they would drop Dean Baquet like a radioactive turd this very day. I can't think of anything more poisonous than a newspaper's executive editor essentially publicly admitting his plan to stoke racial animosity in an effort to influence a presidential election when his charge is to present that publication as an objective deliverer of news. Fulfilling that mission is now impossible."

The bottom line: The 1619 Project is all about ancient history. None of it contributes to healing the country in the present moment. This preoccupation with race only makes it worse. America may not be perfect, but it is as good as it gets. I am reminded of what Muhammad Ali is reported to have told a Soviet reporter: "To me, the USA is still the best country in the world." When Ali returned from a trip to Africa, he remarked, "Thank God my granddaddy got on that boat." I wonder what Ali would say about the 1619 project.

Although Chauvin May Be Guilty, America Is Not

The verdict was read in the Chauvin case: Guilty on all three counts. Police Officer Derek Chauvin was charged with the murder of George Floyd. This section is not about whether or not Chauvin was guilty. I want to focus in on a much larger issue: Is America guilty?

That's what the riots and demonstrations were about: America's guilt or innocence. They were not protesting the outcome of the Chauvin trial. How could they—the verdict was unknown at that time. The riots were all about the trial of the United States of America in the court of public opinion. Make no mistake about it, in that trial the outcome was already decided: Guilty. The protests were based on the assumption that America—*and white America in particular*—is guilty of being a racist, oppressive country. The entire nation has been on trial for systemic racism, police brutality, and white privilege. None of these accusations is based in truth.

The Chauvin/Floyd case is an isolated incident that was blown out of proportion in order to divide the country. "You can't use this as an excuse to destroy America," said radio commentator Mark Levin. Yet that's exactly what the Left wants to do. Floyd and Chauvin have been exploited in order to convince ordinary, law-abiding Americans that the US is a dreadful place that deserves to be taken apart. It began with Obama. From the first day of his presidency, Obama was apologizing all over the world for what he claimed were America's shortcomings and transgressions. Biden, who is nothing more than Obama 2.0, is pushing the same seditious garbage.

Whether they realize it or not, the rioters in our cities were acting in support of critical race theory, the most dangerous ideological movement ever to face our republic. CRT argues that the US suffers from racist oppression of minorities perpetrated by its white citizens. Strange as it may seem, many whites are buying into this abomination.

Half a century after the civil rights movement, whites are not guilty of systemic racism. That's not just my opinion. It is shared by respected black figures such as Thomas Sowell, Shelby Steele, Bob Woodson, and Larry Elder. Biden, who claims to be seeking unity, is fomenting division as he lies about the issue of race.

Having argued that the US is not guilty of being a racist country, let me tell you what we are guilty of. We are guilty of enabling a tsunami of Marxist revolutionary propaganda that is poisoning the very air we breathe. We are guilty of standing by as our children are indoctrinated with self-hate. We are guilty of failing to maintain law and order. Every instance where we allow a riot to occur without consequences is an indictment of how we have abdicated the principles upon which our nation is based.

For that reason, I am despairing of the verdict in the Chauvin case. There is no way he could have received a fair trial. Why do I say that? Because the entire country was threatened with civil anarchy if a "not guilty" verdict came in. The jurors must have been terrified of reprisals if they voted to acquit.

David Horowitz describes the situation in *I Can't Breathe*:

"Because of the mayhem that preceded the trial—the attacks on American cities, the burnings, lootings, and shootings—it strains credulity to believe that a fair trial was even possible. The jury was not sequestered, so that it was well aware of the clamor demanding the 'right verdict' and of the ever-looming threat that there would be hell to pay if any lesser verdict was delivered. There were even specific threats to jurors and witnesses in the case."

Americans sat around with bated breath as the verdict was read because the media convinced us that all hell was about to break loose. Perhaps worst of all are the Democrat politicians who were co-conspirators. Instead of calling for punishment of rioters, Kamala Harris bailed them out. Rep. Maxine Waters encouraged the mob to erupt if she didn't get the verdict she demanded. And finally, the president said he was praying for a guilty verdict.

Yes, America is guilty, but not for being a racist society. America is guilty of repudiating the values on which it was founded.

White is a Color Too

America has come a long way from my childhood on the issue of race. I remember the separate drinking fountains at Woolworth's: "white" and "colored." That would be unthinkable today. In 1963, Dr. King suggested that people should be judged not by their skin color but by their character. The idea made sense and it became a part of the public consciousness. By 2008, it actually looked as though we had transcended America's obsession with skin color.

Instead of signifying that we had arrived at the other end of the race issue, the election of a black president in 2008 set the country back 50 years. Obama's actions in a series of controversial cases stoked the fires of racial discord. Race, says Rep. Mo Brooks, is the new campaign strategy of the Democratic Party: "Divide Americans based on skin pigmentation and try to collect the votes of everybody who is a non-white on the basis that whites are discriminatory and the reason you are where you are in the economic ladder is because of racism."

When the Left advocates diversity and social justice, they want people to be judged by the color of their skin. Under the aegis of identity politics, character becomes irrelevant. Instead of making everyone feel they are part of a unified American social structure, diversity plays into the leftist strategy of "divide and conquer." The Left is achieving the "balkanization" of society, says Mark Levin in *Ameritopia*, "thereby stampeding them in one direction or another as necessary to collapse the existing society or rule over the new one."

Diversity pretends to be inclusive. In reality, it is exclusionary. Diversity implies intolerance of Caucasians and males as it divides Americans between white oppressors and minority victims. As explained by Colin Flaherty in *Don't Make the Black Kids Angry*, racism is the current excuse being offered by the Democrats for the problems afflicting black America. "The ultimate excuse: White racism is everywhere. White racism is permanent. White racism explains everything." The politically correct definition of racism is any criticism of protected classes of people. Evidence in support of the criticism doesn't make it acceptable. According to the PC definition, I am a racist because I have the effrontery to criticize the behavior of minorities.

The latest arrow in the race quiver is the designation, "people of color," which is applied to everyone who is not white. Progressives, says David Horowitz, are using this politically correct term to "further isolate the white European American majority as an oppressor of everyone else."

If you are a person of color, you are exempt from accepted standards of behavior. *New York Times* editorial board member Sarah Jeong, a "woman of color," got away with tweeting "cancel white people." Political commentator Bill O'Reilly said that Jeong's tweets are consistent with the *Times'* editorial philosophy that "white men have destroyed the country."

Rep. Rashida Tlaib has attempted to use her status as a "woman of color" to excuse a series of anti-American and anti-Semitic statements. Tlaib criticized House Speaker Nancy Pelosi for "singling out women of color"—Tlaib and Reps. Omar, Ocasio-Cortez, and Pressley. Tlaib demands that Pelosi "acknowledge the fact that we are women of color, so when you do single us out, be aware of that and what you're doing...because some of us are being singled out in many ways because of our backgrounds..." In other words, you can't criticize people of color, period.

Fortunately, the R word doesn't bite as it did in the 1960s. The accusation of racism is the equivalent of crying wolf. White bullies are no longer running around oppressing everyone else. White institutional racism is an anachronism.

Chapter Three
Identity Politics Encourages Hatred of Whites

In a period rife with scams, the biggest scam of them all is known as *identity politics*. Under the aegis of identity politics, as defined by *Merriam-Webster*, groups having a particular racial, religious, ethnic, social, or cultural identity "promote their own specific interests or concerns without regard to the interests or concerns of any larger political group." These groups are typically divided into oppressors and victims.

"Identity politics," a reader commented on *Amazon*, "has been the driving force behind every single genocide on our planet, including the holocaust." According to identity politics and its associated concept of diversity, people ought to be hired and promoted based on race and gender. Not competence. Not hard work. Not personal sacrifice. The premise of this leftist ideology is that the US is an oppressor nation. Because they are victimized, minorities are in need of special privileges.

Tammy Bruce, in *The New Thought Police*, says that social justice is all about making up for the perceived injustice allegedly perpetrated by heterosexual white males. Minority special interest groups are citing equality, diversity, and social justice as a power grab to impose their agenda on the white majority. Supporters of the social justice movement are not seeking justice, they are seeking control. Blacks who identify as "oppressed" want to trade places with their alleged oppressors.

Identity politics is a fight for equality only in the Orwellian sense. "All animals are equal," George Orwell wrote in *Animal Farm*, "but some animals are more equal than others." We are observing a grab for power by vocal minority groups who want to be more equal than others. If they succeed, they will institutionalize the inquisition against the white population.

White people should not be penalized for their massive contribution to this society, yet that is the goal of identity politics. Our country is strong because it is a meritocracy. Merit—being the best—has always been prized in America. Meritocracy and diversity are opposites. Identity politics is based on the eradication of merit. Minorities are being seduced with a chance at the success and affluence that are possible in America without having to make the effort or personal sacrifices normally needed to obtain them.

The number one reason that some minorities have lagged behind whites is an unwillingness to accept "white" values of hard work, education, and taking responsibility for personal success or failure. "In reality, not everyone makes the same effort," said Jeff Davidson at *Townhall*. "Remember your school classmates who continually slacked off? In the workplace, some people constantly underperform and concurrently seek ever more government benefits. Such people keep voting for Democrats who are skilled at dangling carrots in front of them."

Unfortunately, many people are attracted to identity politics because it offers a less demanding route to success. Where identity politics prevails, you get hired and promoted solely because of your race and gender. What an incredible fantasy! You can breeze through life simply because you are African-American or Hispanic or a woman. It is the kind of fantasy that might appeal to children—winning the big prize through the benefit of wizardry. Somebody waves a magic wand and Harry Potter flies around the room. Children have no conception of the sweat that must be invested to be successful in the adult world. And yet here it is being offered to certain "protected" groups.

A friend sent me a video that pointed out the shortcoming of identity politics. The text from the video was this: "Have you ever boarded a plane and thought to yourself, I hope the pilot is a transgender refugee? Have you ever gone to the emergency room and said, I hope my medical team is incredibly diverse? Have you ever moved to a new city and said, I hope the police department hit its equity goals for the year? If your answer to these questions was NO, if you just wanted the most qualified candidate for the job, you are NORMAL."

Heather Mac Donald, in *The Diversity Delusion: How Race and Gender Pandering Corrupt the University and Undermine Our Culture*, explains that identity politics has taken hold in colleges and universities and is now spreading to the world at large. Companies like Google, Facebook, and United Airlines are showing preferences for minorities and women with little regard for qualifications. White men are being discriminated against on the basis of skin color and gender. Mac Donald warns about the consequences of this trend. China and Russia, she says, are meritocracies. If you are a scientist in China, they don't give a damn about your race or gender. China, for example, caters to top math talent in order to reward effort and achievement, not identity. If the US falls prey to identity politics, we will never be able to compete on the world stage. Within 20 years, the US could easily turn into a third world country.

America's Unhealthy Obsession with Diversity

America is losing its head over diversity. "Sometimes," said economist Thomas Sowell, "it seems as if 'diversity' is going to replace 'the' as the most often used word in the English language." The dictionary definition of diversity is the political and social policy of encouraging tolerance for people of differing backgrounds. Unfortunately, the Left has distorted its meaning. To progressives, diversity means that we must give special privileges to certain protected classes of people, including "people of color" and definitely not whites.

"Diversity in today's America," said Scott Greer, "simply means having fewer whites around." By implying intolerance of Caucasians, diversity is discriminatory and exclusionary. "If you're white, the Left has decided that you are an impediment to diversity," said Jeff Davidson. "The wokesters among us, a highly prejudiced lot, regard all whites as one amorphous mass of people with no individuality, no distinct cultural backgrounds, and indelibly racist."

THE WAR ON WHITES

"Anyone who has been paying attention to corporate culture in America," observed Lynn Uzzell in *RealClearPolitics*, "cannot but have noticed the increasing pressures to 'diversify' the hiring and promotion process, often by explicitly demanding that white (especially white male) employees be held back."

The argument that whites are an inherently flawed group of oppressors is not supportable. The notion that blacks are victims of a white-dominated racist society may have been true prior to the 1960s, but this is a half-century after the civil rights movement.

In their original context, diversity, equity, and inclusion are magnificent words. Unfortunately, the Left has distorted their meaning to signify the complete opposite of the established definitions. The Democratic Party is misusing them to create division, hatred, and exclusion. The most successful accomplishment of the Democrats is what author Mark Levin calls the "balkanization" of society. The Left's objective, Levin says, is to "collapse the existing society" by dividing the people against themselves.

Using its perverted version of diversity, the Democratic Party—under the leadership of Obama—fomented division and hatred after promising just the opposite. The Left's version of diversity goes far beyond tolerance. The basis for diversity policy is that certain groups are encouraged to identify themselves as victims of white people. According to African-American author Thomas Sowell, people on the Left like to say, "I am a victim. Therefore, if you do not give in to my demands, you are a hate-filled, evil person."

Diversity attempts to divide Americans between alleged oppressors—heterosexual, white, Christian males—and "victimized" minorities and women. "To be woke," said Scott McConnell in *The American Conservative*, "is to believe that all social life is permeated by interlocking systems of oppression, and that overturning them is a moral imperative." Instead of making everyone feel they are American, the Obama presidency played into the leftist strategy of "divide and conquer." Obama's destructive vision is coming into full bloom under the Biden/Harris administration.

According special privileges to minorities is the Left's way of marginalizing white people. To progressives, diversity has nothing to do with equality as defined by Dr. Martin Luther King. The Left's version of diversity means that we must give special privileges to certain protected classes of people—people of color, LGBTQ, women—so they can acquire control over the system at the expense of the majority, which at the moment happens to be white. I call this the "tyranny of the minority."

Martin Luther King preached a colorblind society—judge people based on their character, not their skin color. Now the "woke" crowd demands that people be judged by their skin color.

Diversity politics argues for equity. Equity means equality of outcome—everyone enjoys the same income, job success, house, neighborhood, etc. In an equitable world, equal justice under the law is anathema. The law must treat people differently. "The only remedy to past discrimination is present discrimination," argues Ibram X. Kendi in his racist book, *How to Be an Antiracist.* We must give minorities, especially blacks, special treatment in order to even up the scales and compensate for past injustices.

For equity to be achieved, skin color must determine everything. The right kind of skin color is black and brown. White is the wrong color. The same applies to yellow. Asians have been lumped together with whites, probably because they have thrived in America and don't spend their energy complaining. Your kids are having this racist garbage rammed down their throats in our educational system.

The *New York Times* posted Bret Stephens' column entitled, "The New Racism Won't Solve the Old Racism." Stephens writes that the drive for diversity, equity, and inclusion (DEI) "is insulting to everyone who still believes we should be judged by the content of our character." Stephens argues that DEI violates the morality of most Americans by redefining of the word equity—which in common English means the quality of being fair and impartial—to mean something closer to the opposite. "It shouldn't be hard to see that trying to solve the old racism with the new racism will produce only more racism," Stephens concludes. "Justice is never achieved by turning tables."

Eliminating the Meritocracy

Diversity is destroying the critical American value known as meritocracy. Meritocracy and diversity are opposites. Instead of promoting people based on competence, advocates for diversity want promotions to be based on race and gender. With the ascendancy of identity politics, "says

Scott Greer, "skin color trumps merit—as long as that skin isn't white."

Evidence of the trend is everywhere. "Medical schools are discarding traditional standards of merit in order to alter the demographic characteristics of their profession," says Heather Mac Donald. As a direct result, many qualified undergraduates are saying, "Now that I see what is happening in medicine, I will do something else." United Airlines has announced that 50 percent of all new pilots will be chosen from among minorities and women. At 30,000 feet, who wants an affirmative action pilot sitting in the cockpit? Colleges and universities are using a quota system for admission based on race. President Biden has delivered on his promise that the next Supreme Court justice will be black and a woman. Biden did not say, *I'm going to appoint the most competent jurist I can find, and if it happens to be a black woman, that would be good for the country.* He made it clear that he intended to bribe black voters and women by appointing a black woman. No one else need apply.

Where you have obedience to diversity in academia, there is no diversity of thought. People who demand diversity are against viewpoint diversity, also known as free speech. Diversity means "it is great to look different as long as you think the way I do."

"Colleges spend billions of dollars on offices of diversity and inclusion," said Professor Walter Williams. "The last thing that diversity hustlers want is diversity in ideas." Diversity is completely at odds with the most important of American values.

THE WAR ON WHITES

Show business has gone full tilt for diversity. The Walt Disney Company has announced that 50 percent of Disney characters will be LGBTQ or minorities. Eligibility for an Academy Award will no longer be based on merit. Nominees for "best picture" must contain minority themes and have a quota of minorities and women in both cast and crew. Past Oscar winners such as "On the Waterfront," "Patton," and "Lawrence of Arabia" would no longer qualify for an award under the new rules.

The military is losing its combat readiness as the Biden administration demands the inclusion of women in first-line combat units despite evidence that unit effectiveness will be negatively impacted.

The majority of top-25 medical schools are supporting equity and critical race theory. This means that the physician performing your brain surgery could be the product of affirmative action. Going in for surgery will become an act of suicide, as surgeons will no longer be held to "white" standards of excellence.

"The rejection of objective standards of accomplishment is nihilistic," says Heather Mac Donald. "Because of disparate impact, the diversity movement deems color-blind measures of competence to be unjust instruments of racial exclusion." The entire basis of American exceptionalism—competence—will be outlawed.

The government is using diversity to encroach on individual rights and privileges. For example, a new California law mandates that publicly traded companies must include people from "underrepresented communities" on their boards. Do we really want Uncle Sam imposing racial and gender quotas on the business community? The good news is that a Los Angeles court has ruled the law unconstitutional.

America's obsession with diversity makes little sense in view of the tremendous progress that the nation has made since the civil rights movement. As Shelby Steele acknowledged, the oppression of black Americans has been relegated to history. The bitter allegations of critical race theory and Black Lives Matter cannot be justified. "In Baltimore, where Freddie Gray died," said black talk radio host Larry Elder, "the majority of the city council is black, the top cop is black, the number two cop is black, the majority of the command staff is black, the mayor is black, the AG is black, and yet here we are talking about racism. It's absurd."

In addition to fomenting racial strife, diversity encourages minorities not to take responsibility for their own lives. This is part of the Democratic Party's plan to make as many people as possible dependent on government handouts. Entitlements foster a victim mentality that places the blame on whites.

Giving special treatment to any one group is in violation of the equal protection clause. It is also the worst kind of racism. Blaming current social problems on alleged white oppression heightens racial tensions and keeps the country divided. That seems to be what the Democrats want.

THE WAR ON WHITES

Implicit Bias—the New Password of Identity Politics

Identity politics has given rise to catastrophic social division that is busy destroying the legacy of Martin Luther King and the civil rights movement. Where identity politics prevails, you get hired and promoted because of your race and gender and for no other reason. To sell that radical concept to the public, a new password has been introduced into the vernacular: *implicit bias.*

Implicit bias refers to omnipresent racist attitudes that allegedly exist on the level of the unconscious, beyond our conscious awareness or intentional control. "Despite our best intentions and without our awareness," according to *vox.com,* "racial stereotypes and assumptions creep into our minds and affect our actions. That's why implicit racial bias has been called *the new diversity paradigm*—one that recognizes the role that bias plays in the day-to-day functioning of all human beings."

Whether you realize it or not, if you are white, you are automatically guilty of racism because of your skin color. If you doubt that you are a racist, it is proof you are a racist. That is the thesis of the implicit bias handbook, known as *White Fragility.* As one anonymous critic wrote, this insidious work is a "book for those that need more of a reason to feel bad about themselves." Schools and companies are ordering it by the boatload. It is required reading for young people who cannot defend themselves and adults who are afraid of losing their jobs.

91

Implicit bias forms the basis for critical race theory, which is the view that the US is inherently racist, that minorities and women are oppressed by whites and especially by white men, and that white people achieve their economic and political objectives at the expense of people of color. CRT argues that racism is present in every aspect of life; that all alternative theories are racist; and that anyone who disagrees is racist (even if they are black). It rejects science and Western Civilization as products of white racism.

Implicit bias allegedly proves the existence of systemic racism, even though respected black figures such as Thomas Sowell, Shelby Steele, Bob Woodson, and Larry Elder are unanimous in their agreement that the oppression of blacks is a thing of the past. Rather than exhibiting systemic racism, white Americans have taken important steps to make life better for blacks. You can't have affirmative action AND systemic racism. Don't tell the adherents of CRT.

There is no acceptable defense when you are accused of implicit bias. If you are white, you have it. "It's a disease borne from the hateful halls of leftwing academia," says Fox's Greg Gutfeld, who adds:

"Critical race theory undermines the positive core beliefs of America by redefining the nation as an engine of oppression. What you're seeing on America's city streets are its results. Starting on campus, then leaking into unconscious bias training at work—culminating in infantile rioters who use this ideology to justify violence. Do you wonder why these clones accost people at restaurants? They've been brainwashed to think you're

'unconsciously racist' and they're going to wake you up. 'Unconsciously racist' means even when you say you aren't racist, the response is, 'Well, you just aren't conscious of it.'"

Affirmative Action—Yes or No?

Affirmative action has a divisive effect on society. "Far and away the most egregious form of government interference with the contractual rights of private persons and organizations is carried out in the name of affirmative action," says Richard Pipes in *Property and Freedom.* "Initially conceived as a means of enforcing principles of nondiscrimination in regard to black citizens... [affirmative action] was soon extended to other groups and ultimately turned into a vehicle for reverse discrimination against whites and males."

Qualified white job candidates are regularly passed over for minority candidates with fewer qualifications. For example, Heather Mac Donald found that blacks and Hispanics are promoted ahead of whites in the New York Police Department. "Blacks and Hispanics became detectives almost five years earlier than whites and took half the time as whites did to be appointed to deputy inspector or deputy chief."

A UCLA study revealed that colleges that allow racial preferences give blacks more than a 5-1 advantage over whites in the admission process. "Students are encouraged in their application to indicate that they are nonwhite in order to gain entry," says Scott Greer.

Unfortunately, it does not always do justice to the intended beneficiaries. Blacks, the strongest defenders of affirmative action, can suffer negative consequences from racial preferences. Affirmative action recipients at colleges and universities experience a high dropout rate. *Mismatch theory* describes the many minority students who are accepted at schools beyond their aptitude, creating a sense of failure, depression, and alienation. "The students struggle academically because they got into a school that was beyond their skill level thanks to racial preferences in college admissions," Greer explains. "Instead of blaming a system that judges them by their skin color, or their own failures to study, they blame the invisible systemic racism of the schools they attend for why their grades aren't so great."

Attorney and former Harvard professor Alan Dershowitz brings up another negative outcome of affirmative action at universities—it is anti-white. He says it is a "zero-sum game," meaning that if the number of blacks admitted to Harvard is raised by affirmative action, the number of whites has to decline. For example, if 200 more blacks are admitted, 200 fewer whites will be accepted. The solution, Dershowitz says, is for Harvard to increase the size of the class so that the number of whites will remain the same—but they refuse to do that. The result is that many deserving white students are denied admission to the college of their choice as a direct result of affirmative action.

In *The Diversity Delusion*, Heather Mac Donald describes the history of affirmative action at California universities, which offers an accurate view of what is taking place nationally. In 1996, California passed Proposition 209, where the state's voters chose to ban race and gender preferences. The California university system went bananas—Prop 209 contradicted its commitment to diversity, which became a euphemism for using race and gender criteria for admission. "California," said Mac Donald, "shows what happens when [diversity] comes into conflict with the law." Diversity wins. Government and university bureaucrats don't really give a damn about what the public wants. In the case of California, the university system simply found a way to disregard the law.

The California university system did everything possible to ignore Prop 209. They were very clever about it. Instead of confessing that admissions were based on race and sex, they began diluting their academic requirements and ignoring the objective academic rankings of applicants so that more minority students would qualify for admission. For example, a minority student who was number one in his class at a low-ranked high school might be given preference over the number one white student from an academically competitive school.

The results were predictable: the affirmative action students met with failure. One Berkeley professor confessed that "they admitted people who could barely read. There was a huge drop-out rate of affirmative action admits by mid-terms. No one had taught them the need to go to class. So we started introducing BS majors, in an effort to make the university ready for them, rather than making them ready for the university." According to the *Los Angeles Times*, racial preferences are not just ill advised, "they are positively sadistic."

"For the preference lobby," Mac Donald concludes, "a failing diversity student is better than no diversity student at all—because the game is not about the students but about the self-image of the institution that so beneficently extends its largesse to them." The same thing can be said of the Biden administration and its equity agenda (see Chapter Six).

One of the saddest outcomes of affirmative action is that minority hires suffer from the suspicion that they were selected based on equity concerns rather than competence.

Qualified People Don't Need Affirmative Action

The hiring obstacles to minorities that existed 50 years ago have been swept away. In today's job market, if people of color are not hired in greater numbers it is not because of racism, but because they don't meet the job qualifications. In *When Race Trumps Merit*, Heather Mac Donald drives home that diversity is stymied by the relative lack of qualified blacks. She cites the example of blacks in STEM fields. In response to the argument that bias drives the lack of blacks, she points out that "there are simply not enough black STEM PhDs to go around." Blacks account for only 1 percent of all physics doctorates, 3.2 percent of all mathematics doctorates, 3.4 percent in computer science, 3.5 percent in chemistry, 4.2 percent in engineering and NONE in medical or atmospheric physics, logic, number theory, robotics or structural engineering. The same proportions can be found in the legal profession and the corporate arena.

A qualified black or Hispanic person has no difficulty finding a job. Employers are jumping out of their shorts for a chance to hire minority applicants. "One would have difficulty finding an elite institution today that does not pressure its managers to hire and promote as many blacks and Hispanics as possible," Mac Donald said. This is especially true in our universities. "There is not a single faculty that is not desperately trying to find underrepresented minorities or women to hire." Why do you suppose they have so many diversity executives?

Competent black applicants are guaranteed a job. If I were black, I would have a field day. Book contracts, speeches, whatever. As it is, I'm stuck with my white privilege and, frankly, it ain't what it used to be.

If you are a qualified person of color, you don't need affirmative action. Only unqualified people need affirmative action. Affirmative action means lowering standards. That is why Biden's equity plan will fail. Federal agencies will be forced to lower standards in order to hire unqualified applicants and the quality of our government will sink even lower than it is now.

Arguments for affirmative action omit the question of why minorities need racial or gender preferences in the first place. Students are not rejected for admission to elite universities because they are the wrong race, but due to inadequate educational preparation and lack of family support for education as a worthwhile goal. Affirmative action doesn't work because it fails to address either of those issues.

Another major shortcoming of affirmative action is the implication that minorities are inferior and therefore unable to achieve without special assistance. "When you give racial preference to the child of two black professionals with advanced degrees and six-figure incomes," says Shelby Steele, "as entrée to a university that has not discriminated against blacks in more than sixty years—then you are clearly implying an inherent and irremediable black inferiority."

The Left would like to see our standards lowered across the board, which would "level the playing field" and reduce our competitiveness in the world. Should we seek social justice by lowering the standards to the lowest denominator via affirmative action, or should we require the lowest denominator—minority students, for example—to meet the higher standard? Lowering standards has given us an educational system that is producing substandard results. Statistics that show the US lagging behind in educational accomplishments are proof that the Left is succeeding.

The group that suffers the most from affirmative action, says Scott Greer, is lower-income whites. "Without the financial resources and the proper skin color to get into a good four-year university, millions of poor whites are denied their opportunity at the American Dream."

Sociologist Nathan Glazer argued in his 1975 book, *Affirmative Discrimination*, that affirmative action is a form of reverse racism violating white people's right to equal protection under the law. But the Supreme Court's decision in *Regents of the University of California v. Bakke* (1978) said that while racial quotas for minority students were discriminatory toward white people, the use of racial preferences to accept more minority applicants is constitutional. Quotas bad, affirmative action good. Confusing? Without a doubt.

THE WAR ON WHITES

"Affirmative action," says Shelby Steele in *White Guilt: How Blacks and Whites Together Destroyed the Promise of the Civil Rights Era*, "explicitly violates many [American] principles—equal protection under the law, meritorious advancement—that the King-era civil rights movement fought for." Conservatives, by and large, believe that affirmative action based on membership in a designated racial group is a threat to individualism and meritocracy.

Affirmative action is not enforced in the NBA, whose players are 74 percent black. All that matters is how well you play basketball. For the same reason, merit ought to be applied to airline pilots, Marines, and brain surgeons. When I am flying over the Pacific Ocean, I want the most qualified pilot sitting at the controls. As a former Marine, I appreciate that combat units should not have their standards lowered simply to accommodate women or transgenders. When I am being operated on for a brain tumor, I don't want to look up and see the winner of this year's social justice award.

Many on the Left dismiss the arguments against affirmative action. Sociologist Eduardo Bonilla-Silva described anti–affirmative action and 'reverse racism' attitudes as part of a "mean-spirited white racial animus." Anastasia Reesa Tomkin, in her article, "The Case for Selective Discrimination," *Nonprofit Quarterly*, Nov. 18, 2021, seems to agree. Tomkin writes:

"If the law states that people are protected from racial discrimination, does this apply to white people, even though they have been the benefactors of white supremacy? Is whiteness a protected class the same as

any other? You see, we can't simply shift to colorblind rhetoric after decades of heavily prioritizing white people in every way possible and expect that this would produce the racial equity that Dr. King dreamed of. The generational wealth gap, for one, will not change if we only avoid creating policies that explicitly disadvantage Black people. There would need to be reparations, a thorough analysis of the existing policies, and perhaps a variety of programs specifically designed for black people's benefit. If some white people are not replaced by people of color in leadership positions, there won't be diverse leadership. If people of color are not hired, there won't be diverse staff. Amending the insidious discrimination of the past to any significant degree will not be achieved through neutrality or colorblindness. It will be achieved through prioritizing and empowering those who have been disempowered and sidelined for so long. It will require a host of racially conscious measures, one of which could well be selective discrimination. After centuries of pro-white ideology being enforced through terrorism, intimidation, and the rule of law, humane and moral "pro-color" initiatives are the only practical solution. The dethroning of white supremacy is integral to racial equity."

The argument for affirmative action is that blacks have been disadvantaged for so long that giving them special privilege is necessary to make up for past discrimination and "white privilege." The refutation of that argument is that two wrongs don't make a right. "Dethroning" whites is neither equitable nor practical. The unfair conditions of 100 years ago do not justify discrimination in the present. Contrary to what Ibram X. Kendi says, past discrimination can't be remedied by present discrimination.

Diversity proponents say, "If people of color are not hired, there won't be a diverse staff." This is the problem with diversity. Diversity for its own sake is a misguided goal—bringing minorities up to meeting standards of excellence ought to be what we aim for. Hiring people who are qualified. Equity in the truest sense means leveling the playing field in the present by means of a meritocracy where everyone is judged by the same standards, not giving one team an advantage because the players had a rough childhood.

Again I quote Shelby Steele: "Past oppression cannot be conflated into present-day oppression." And Bret Stephens: "It shouldn't be hard to see that trying to solve the old racism with the new racism will produce only more racism. Justice is never achieved by turning tables."

Steele offers an intriguing reason why many whites are in favor of affirmative action. "Whites and American institutions live by a simple formula," Steele says, "lessening responsibility for minorities equals moral authority; increasing it equals racism. This is the formula that locks many whites into publicly supporting affirmative action even as they privately dislike it."

White Guilt

A perplexing question I have tried to answer is, why did so many whites vote for Obama? Here are four answers.

Reason number one: They didn't like John McCain. I can understand that. I didn't like McCain either but felt more secure voting for someone with a verifiable track record instead of a candidate who went to great lengths to keep his background hidden. Obama had no record of any kind that I could determine. "This is a man who has actually accomplished nothing other than advancing his career through rhetoric," said Thomas Sowell. "It reminds me of a sophomore in college who thinks that he can run the world because he's never had to run anything." That didn't work for me.

Reason number two: Obama was charismatic and made all sorts of promises to reunite the country. People who voted for him told me they believed that a black man and a reformer would improve race relations, open up new avenues of dialogue with Iran and Syria, and undo the mess created by George W. Bush in Iraq. His campaign slogan, "Hope and change," was brilliant—not because of what it meant but because of what it did not mean. All by itself, it didn't mean a damn thing. It was pure nonsense on purpose. Obama never really said what it meant. The brilliance lay in the way it was interpreted. He won votes because voters believed it meant what they wanted it to mean, not what Obama wanted it to mean.

If you were a voter, you could begin a sentence with "Hope and change" and finish it any way you liked according to your own political leanings. People did not suspect that Obama's idea of change was to turn America upside down.

Reason number three: They didn't want to be labeled a racist. I can relate to that. Calling someone a racist today is the equivalent of calling someone a "pinko" during the McCarthy era. A group of acquaintances levelled the R word against me in 2008 when they discovered I was not voting for their hero. It was upsetting—but merely confirmed my decision not to vote for him.

Reason number four: White guilt. You are guilty of racism until you are proven innocent. White guilt is a powerful shaming force that many believe was responsible for the election of Obama. Many white people who voted for him did so out of a subconscious desire to virtue-signal, to prove that they are not racist, to prove that America is worthy of respect and admiration rather than condemnation.

Stripped down to its essence, white guilt is an effort by white liberals to feel better about themselves, not to atone for a moral crime. Scott Greer defines it:

"Instead of white skin serving as a marker for superior values, it's a sign of inheriting a multitude of past injustices. No matter your actions, background, or beliefs, you carry the burden of European oppression if you are white. White guilt is the collective shame all white people must share for the past crimes of a few long-dead Caucasians against other groups. This is the new white man's burden. The basis for white guilt is acceptance of the premise of left-wing intellectual Susan Sontag: 'The

white race is the cancer of human history.' Upon accepting that notion, whites must strive for atonement from all the groups they have wronged. The feeling of superiority driven in by white supremacy is replaced with a state of utter shame under white guilt. The only kind of racial discussions whites should engage in are ones where they sit down, shut up, and allow their moral superiors to berate them." (I'm sure Robin DiAngelo would agree with this description. See Chapter Five.)

Shelby Steele explains it in *White Guilt*:

"The great power of white guilt comes from the fact that it functions by stigma, like racism itself. Whites and American institutions are stigmatized as racist until they prove otherwise. White guilt depends on their fear of stigmatization, their fear of being called a racist. Thus, white guilt is nothing less than a social imperative that all whites, from far-left socialists to Republican presidents, are accountable to. Today, the white West— like Germany after the Nazi defeat—lives in a kind of secular penitence in which the slightest echo of past sins brings down a withering condemnation. There is now a cloud over white skin where there once was unquestioned authority. I call this white guilt not because it is a guilt of conscience but because people stigmatized with moral crimes—here racism and imperialism—lack moral authority and so act guiltily whether they feel guilt or not. They struggle, above all else, to dissociate themselves from the past sins they are stigmatized with. When they

behave in ways that invoke the memory of those sins, they must labor to prove that they have not relapsed into their group's former sinfulness."

Steele goes on to explain what he sees as the real purpose of black militancy:

"Black militancy came into existence solely to exploit white guilt as a pressure on white America to take more responsibility for black advancement. Effectively, black militancy and white guilt are two sides of the same coin. Their goal is always to redistribute responsibility for black uplift from blacks themselves to American institutions. So black militancy, for all its bluster of black pride and its rhetoric of self-determination, is a mask worn always and only for the benefit of whites. Black militancy became, in fact, a militant belief in white power and a correspondently militant denial of black power."

Steele's words explain how white guilt accounts for the Biden administration's focus on mandating special privileges for people of color. Mark Levin has raised the question, why do so many affluent whites buy into identity politics? The answer is white guilt. Many whites have fallen for the defamatory argument that they do not deserve their white privilege. They feel constrained to prove that they are different from the average white person. This may account for the current crusade to enforce diversity at all levels of society.

If white guilt becomes an unchallenged dogma, hate against whites will increase as nonwhites are told to blame their failures in life on white supremacy, and are taught to see Western history as one long tale of oppression. Eventually there will be a white backlash. That is part of the Left's program. A civil war between races and ethnic groups is entirely possible. It is happening now in France between native-born French and Muslim immigrants. It can happen to us.

How can identity politics be defeated if even whites are being sucked in? The good news is that not all whites or minorities are drinking the Kool-Aid. Half the country voted for Donald Trump because the allure of identity politics is not as strong as the Left would like it to be.

Diversity Executives—The US Version of Soviet Political Commissars

In the thrilling submarine movie, *The Hunt for Red October*, the authority of Russian sub captain Sean Connery is challenged by the political officer whose job is to ensure that the sub is run in accordance with Soviet party ideology. The man's interference becomes so aggravating that Connery's character kills him. We are facing a similar threat from an avalanche of diversity executives.

A political commissar or political officer is responsible for ideological conformity in military units to ensure party control of the unit. Political commissars were heavily used in the Soviet Red Army, as well as in the armed forces of Nazi

Germany. The US can now be added to the list with its battalions of diversity officers.

Diversity, equity, and inclusion (DEI) executives—our political commissars—are tasked with enforcing anti-white leftist policies in corporations, universities, and government agencies. They do not contribute to the competent functioning of those institutions and in fact may detract from their profitability and efficiency. An article in *The Economist* suggested that 12 of the most terrifying words in the English language are, "I'm from human resources, and I'm here to organize a diversity workshop."

Employing significant numbers of diversity executives is all the rage. In 2020, DEI was a $3.4 billion industry. The average university, for example, now has 45.1 people dedicated to promoting diversity on campus. The University of Michigan has a whopping 163 diversity officers. That's 2.3 diversity officers for every one member of its history faculty. Is it any wonder that college tuition has skyrocketed?

Stanford Law School offers a good example of how DEI executives can be counterproductive by interfering with the diversity of ideas. The school's diversity, equity, and inclusion dean, Tirien A. Steinbach, encouraged students to prevent a federal judge from speaking at a university function. Court of Appeals Judge Stuart Kyle Duncan was invited by the student chapter of the conservative Federalist Society to address the student body at the prestigious law school. The judge was targeted by a group of leftist students because of his ruling on a transgender pedophile in 2020, where he refused to allow her bid to get her name changed.

The protestors claimed the judge had committed crimes against women, gays, blacks, and trans people.

Justice Duncan was repeatedly shouted down and drowned out by the angry students who screamed that they hoped Duncan's daughters would be raped. He was unable to give his prepared remarks. The behavior of the protesting students was a clear violation of the school's free speech policy.

Adding to the insanity was an impromptu lecture by diversity officer Steinbach, who obviously does not believe in diversity of ideas. Instead of calming the students down so that Justice Duncan could exercise free speech, Steinbach piously lectured him for six minutes. She asserted that free speech did not justify giving Duncan a platform and scolded him for doing "harm" with his rulings. Steinbach deliberately subverted a critical takeaway for law students, namely learning how to be aware of opposing points of view. This does not bode well for the kind of lawyers that Stanford will be turning out.

"The DEI training programs will tell individuals who are white that they are inherently guilty of some sort of acts committed in the past by people of their same ethnicity, and so that somehow they must carry some sort of guilt around with them," said Jonathan Butcher of *The Heritage Foundation*. "Because of that, the DEI officers on campus, they're not really talking about diversity—what they're actually doing is limiting the number of ideas that can be discussed in lecture halls and in classrooms." That describes what happened at Stanford.

THE WAR ON WHITES

Can it truly be said that Stanford is better off for employing a diversity dean? Steinbach has contributed to the demise of Stanford Law's reputation. This is an example of how our institutions are being harmed by their reliance on DEI commissars.

Another disturbing example involved the Pentagon's diversity chief, Kelisa Wing. Wing made a series of racist statements about white people. "I'm exhausted with these white folx," she wrote. "[T]his lady actually had the CAUdacity to say that black people can be racist too... I had to stop the session and give Karen the BUSINESS... [W]e are not the majority, we don't have power," Wing said in a tweet. *Caudacity* is a slang term that is applied to white people. "If another Karen tells me about her feelings," Wing wrote, "I might lose it."

Wing was appointed as diversity, equity and inclusion chief at the Pentagon's education section, which services over 60,000 military-connected children at 160 schools around the globe. As reported by *Fox News*, Wing stated that her goal was to "tear down the system" in education. She asserted that it is time for a "racial reckoning" and "revolution." In response, Rep. Elise Stefanik, who sits on the House Armed Services Committee, said, "This woke ideology is destroying our military and poisoning the minds of American children." Wing and other diversity commissars attempt to justify their divisive racist behavior by cloaking it under the banner of diversity.

ED BRODOW

DEI Initiatives Have Failed

After all the hullabaloo, DEI initiatives have not been successful. "It shouldn't be surprising that most diversity programs aren't increasing diversity," reports the *Harvard Business Review*. "Laboratory studies show that this kind of force-feeding can activate bias rather than stamp it out. In analyzing three decades' worth of data from more than 800 US firms and interviewing hundreds of line managers and executives at length, we've seen that companies get better results when they ease up on the control tactics."

A Harvard study concluded that mandatory diversity training in corporations tends to trigger bias and backlash against minorities. Five years after diversity training, the share of black women and Asian managers actually decreased in the firms they looked at.

Harvard organizational sociology professor Frank Dobbin found that for white women, and for black men and women in management positions, diversity programs made things worse. He concluded that the companies he studied would actually employ more women and black men today if they had never had diversity training at all.

"I did not find one single study," said a Harvard professor interviewed by John Stossel, "which has found that diversity training leads to more diversity."

It is difficult to extract candid confessions of humiliation from white employees who have been through anti-white trainings, as they are afraid of being fired. That's exactly what happened to a brave Google engineer after he composed an anti-diversity "manifesto" protesting DEI training, referring to it as "just a lot of shaming." The company fired him. He has since hit back, suing Google for discrimination against conservative white males.

One woman called diversity trainings "a convenient tactic of beating up on white people which is growing in popularity. As someone who came to that event willing to champion the cause of diversity," she said, "I felt betrayed."

Erec Smith gave up his job as diversity officer at Drew University. When asked why he quit, he replied, "I just thought it was a useless thing. There is a better way to go about this. It seems to be doing worse. It seems to be making people less likely to interact with people who are unlike them."

"Has academia gone insane?" Smith was asked. "Yes," he replied, "It has gone insane. If you wanted to hold down a group of people without them knowing it, this woke thing is a good strategy."

DEI initiatives are being seen by many as a form of racial blackmail. Corporations have paid hundreds of millions of dollars to avoid a racist stigma. Shelby Steele recounts the story of a Texaco executive who was overheard making a remark some interpreted as racist. Texaco paid $750 million—that's right, *million*—to what Steele calls "the corrupt diversity industry" even though the executive in question was found to have merely repeated a nonracist term he picked up at a company-sponsored diversity training program.

DEI jobs seem to be on the way out. "Biden's incompetent, identity-obsessed administration has ironically caused a mediocre economy that is leading businesses to shed DEI jobs," reported Zachary Faria in the *Washington Examiner.* "DEI layoffs have been most prominent in the technology industry. And universities are being forced to put the woke genie back in the bottle in states such as Florida and Texas, as Republican governors and legislators rightfully focus on tearing down bloated DEI bureaucracies that run rampant through college administrations."

As Bret Stephens said, "Justice is never achieved by turning tables." Justice is never achieved by hiring boatloads of diversity commissars.

Biden Wants Equity

Biden is demanding that all federal agencies submit to equity. The objective of equity is not equality of opportunity, but rather equality of outcome. We must give minorities, especially blacks, special treatment in order to even up the scales and compensate for past injustices. Equity means affirmative action in employment and college admissions. Equity in housing and neighborhoods. Equity in compensation.

A prime example of "equity" in action is occurring in Virginia, where several high schools in Fairfax and Loudoun Counties have withheld National Merit awards from deserving students in order to avoid hurting the feelings of those not awarded. As reported in *The Federalist,* "Asian-American students are highly represented among the recipients, and some believe withholding the awards to be an act of racially motivated biases against Asian students. The withholding of awards from children is par for the course in the war against merit to ensure equal outcomes." Fairfax County also uses "equity grading," where under-served students can be given preference.

Another example of equity is the demand that first dibs on the COVID vaccine should go to "people of color," and definitely not to Caucasians. The science tells us that older people should get the vaccine first because they are the most vulnerable, but no, equity says that blacks don't have equal access to healthcare so they should get the vaccine first. In other words, skin color—not science—should determine how healthcare is apportioned.

I googled equity. Here is what it said: equality achieves fairness through treating everyone the same regardless of need, while equity achieves this through treating people differently dependent on need. That is a lie. Equity has nothing to do with need. Equity attempts to achieve its concept of fairness by treating people differently based on their skin color. For equity to be achieved, skin color must determine everything. The right kind of skin color is black and brown. White is the wrong color. Harvard, Yale, and Stanford are marching in tune with this nonsense.

The problem with equality of outcome is that it can never be accomplished without control by a coercive centralized authority. "A free society will not be one of equality," said James Peron, author of *Exploding Population Myths*. "Even if we were able to distribute all wealth equally, once the heavy hand of centralized control was removed, inequality would immediately result. The destruction of freedom is the only method for implementing equality of results."

Equity brings with it two dubious travel companions: critical race theory and cancel culture. Both would have been right at home in Nazi Germany. Critical race theory categorizes you as either oppressor or oppressed based on your race, gender, or sexual orientation. To accept critical race theory, one must acknowledge the existence of systemic racism and white privilege. If you question either of them, it proves you are a racist. "That notion reflects the true nature of all leftist ideology by being ultimately authoritarian in nature," writes Eleanor Krasne in *heritage.org*. "You either agree with the left's worldview or you are an enemy of all that is good."

You can see how equity and critical race theory go hand in hand. Anyone who attended college during or after the 1960s, says Krasne, has been sucked into this web of deceit. If you refuse to buy in, you automatically become fodder for the cancel culture. The *New York Post* has described cancel culture as "the phenomenon of promoting the banishing of people, brands and even shows and movies due to what some consider to be offensive or problematic remarks or ideologies."

No one is immune. Even someone as successful as Harry Potter author J.K. Rowling has been subject to the cancel culture for allegedly making anti-trans comments. If Rowling can be cancelled, so can you. Rowling is in a much better position to cope than the average person, who is at risk of losing his job and reputation.

THE WAR ON WHITES

Critical race theory is unapologetically anti-white. The campaign for equity has reinforced the inquisition against white people. Never in my wildest dreams did I foresee this. Are you ready to apologize for your skin color and surrender everything you've worked for to other people based solely on their skin color? You better...or else the cancel culture will be coming for you.

United's New "Woke" Hiring Policy Is Racist and Sexist

My speaking schedule requires a lot of airline travel. Based on where I live, the best routes are on United Airlines. I was upset to learn United has announced that its new hiring process for pilots will be based on racial and gender quotas rather than the most competent person for the job.

"Our flight deck should reflect the diverse group of people on board our planes every day," the airline tweeted. "Over the next decade," said United CEO Scott Kirby, "United will train 5,000 pilots who will be guaranteed a job with United—and our plan is for half of them to be women and people of color." From the sound of it, one might infer that United has no women or minorities on the flight deck. According to *Newsweek*, United acknowledges that 20 percent of its current pilot population is composed of women and people of color.

What is an acceptable percentage? Should there even be such a thing as an acceptable percentage? Heather Mac Donald is concerned about what happens when we promote the idea of acceptable percentages based on race:

"Any institution today that has racial disparities in its demographics is considered to be racist per se. That's the only allowable explanation for racial disparities. As long as racism is the only allowable explanation for why Google's engineers are not 13 per cent black or why the physics department at Harvard University is not 13 per cent black, then these institutions are under threat."

United Airlines evidently is more concerned about being considered racist than it is about maintaining airline safety.

According to *Western Journal News*, United is receiving substantial backlash from angry customers. *"When I'm 31,000 feet in the air,"* tweeted one frequent flyer, *"I'm not really gonna find comfort in knowing that my pilot was an affirmative action hire."*

Another tweeted, *"Men and white people don't deserve discrimination because of their sex or race. Its sick that you're proud of this."*

A third person tweeted, *"'Diversity over skill and safety' is one hell of a slogan for an airline."*

Conservative author Brigitte Gabriel tweeted, *"They are literally putting the lives of their customers at risk in the name of being woke."*

A typical tweet in support of United's decision read like this: *"When folks claim only white males are qualified to fly a jumbo jet, that's racism. Diverse doesn't mean unqualified."* The error in this kind of thinking is that no one has claimed that only white men are qualified as pilots. Nor has anyone claimed that minorities or women are unqualified. It is not racism to suggest that pilots should be chosen from the most qualified applicants, regardless of race or sex. In fact, it used to be known as common sense until the woke crowd got their hands on it.

United says it wants its pilots to reflect the racial and sex makeup of the passengers. What happens if the plane is 90 percent full of white men? Do they kick off the female pilot and bring in a man from the bull pen (no pun intended)? What if most of the passengers are under ten years old? Does United have a room full of juvenile pilots in readiness? Questions like these expose the absurdity of race and sex-based criteria.

Hiring quotas based on race and gender violate basic notions of fairness and meritocracy. Such quotas are, in short, racist and sexist. You cannot say in the same breath that giving preference to white males is racist and sexist but giving preference to women and minorities is not. It has to work both ways. United is succumbing to critical race theory, which argues that women and minorities have been oppressed and therefore it is justified to give them preference. Liberals want to judge everything based on race and gender. CRT and the allied notion of "equity" seek to abolish the important American value known as meritocracy. Using merit as the primary job criterion is responsible for our success as a nation. If we lose it, we lose everything.

A good example of how "equity" is distorted can be found at the Academy Awards. No longer will a film be judged based on its artistic merit. Beginning next year, in order to qualify for a Best Picture Oscar, a movie must demonstrate it is practicing equity by having at least 50 percent women and minorities in its cast and crew. Classic Best Picture winners of the past such as *Casablanca, Gone with the Wind, Lawrence of Arabia, Hamlet, On the Waterfront,* and *The Sound of Music* would be disqualified under the new rules. What about a Spike Lee film composed mostly of blacks? Would that qualify? Or would it be kicked out because it lacked a sufficient percentage of white actors in the cast? I doubt it— for the simple reason that CRT doesn't work both ways.

Sadly, United has joined a growing list of woke corporations—Coca-Cola, Delta Airlines, Starbucks, and Nike, just to name a few—whose weak managements have succumbed to the new liberal playbook. It does not bode well for our country.

By facilitating identity politics, says Scott Greer, college campuses are a preview of future social and political discourse. "The kids marching today to shut down a speaker they don't like could very well be the senators, judges, and newspaper editors of tomorrow." Our country could be run by people who believe in extreme identity politics. Good luck with that.

Chapter Four
Complicity of the Educational System

The Left has infiltrated our educational system, causing it to support the demonization of whites. Students are taught that self-hate is appropriate if you happen to be Caucasian. Anything created by whites is to be considered racist and ought to be struck down. The use of standard English is racist. Math is racist. White skin is racist.

"The education system has been weaponized by the radical left to push an anti-American agenda," said former teacher Douglas Blair at *The Daily Signal*. "The left uses a combination of propaganda and suppression to push kids into the ensnaring grip of socialism and anti-patriotism. Conservatives must demand an end to the indoctrination of our youth or face a new American public taught since childhood that the country shouldn't exist."

"Across the nation," reports *Real Clear Education*, "parents have pushed back on teachers promoting a leftist political agenda in K-12 classrooms, from the purported teaching of forms of critical race theory to documented evidence of politically charged rhetoric, such as one educator in Sparta, Wisconsin, calling conservatives 'ignorant and poor.'"

A distraught mother told the audience of Dr. Phil's TV show that a California high school is teaching critical race theory—without her consent—to her daughter, who is of mixed white and Latino heritage. Explaining that members of her family have different complexions, the mother said that she and her more tanned-skinned daughter were labeled as oppressed, while the other half of the family—the sister, the brother, the father—are oppressors. An excellent example of how absurd CRT has become.

Because of her skin color, said the daughter, she was taught that she would never be as successful as her white peers. A former California teacher confirmed that the schools are indoctrinating kids into believing that America was "built to only help the white man and to oppress everybody else. It is dividing America based on race." This is how non-whites are being brainwashed to hate whites.

Biden's Department of Education recently proposed using millions of dollars in taxpayer funds to provide grants exclusively to American schools that teach critical race theory and the 1619 Project. "Countless schools across America already utilize these radical, dangerous projects in their curriculum," according to *amac.us*, "and the Biden administration wants to provide American schools that haven't already implemented these ideas into their curriculum with a direct financial incentive to do so."

Heather Mac Donald, in *The Diversity Delusion*, describes what has happened to American education:

"A charged set of ideas now dominate higher education: that human beings are defined by their skin color, sex, and sexual preference; that discrimination based on those characteristics has been the driving force in

Western civilization; and that America remains a profoundly bigoted place, where heterosexual white males continue to deny opportunity to everyone else. These ideas, which may be subsumed under the categories of 'diversity' and identity politics, have remade the university. Diversity—meaning socially engineered racial proportionality—is now the official ideology of the education behemoth."

How bad is the situation in higher ed? A study by the UCLA Higher Education Research Institute found that 62.7 percent of full-time faculty at four-year colleges and universities identify as liberal or far left. Only 11.9 percent identify as conservative or far right. Another poll pegged liberals at 87 percent and conservatives at 13 percent. In some schools, the ratio of Democrats to Republicans can be as high as 20-1. A recent study identified Democrats to Republicans in journalism departments of 1,500 universities at 20-1 and a whopping 33.5-1 in history departments.

How did campuses become fueling stations for the Left? According to Ben Shapiro in *Bullies*, college administrators decided in the 1960s that it was "easier to appease rampaging leftist students than to deal with them. They came to an agreement with the wildebeests: stop taking over the buildings and locking the doors, and we'll start teaching you about how America sucks."

Gradually that translated into liberalism becoming a prerequisite for getting hired. Many campuses require new faculty members to sign a "diversity statement." They are forced to pledge allegiance to the college's leftist agenda, said

Professor Walter Williams. "What diversity oaths seek," he said, "is to maintain political conformity among the faculty indoctrinating our impressionable, intellectually immature young people." Part of that indoctrination is marginalization of white people.

The leftist agenda on campus is heavy on bashing whites. "The momentum of the present is veering toward tribalism, not unity," says Scott Greer. "And the only thing keeping the tribes of the Left unified right now is their shared animosity toward whites." Greer offers numerous examples of anti-white protests by black student groups, some of which are hard to believe. An example is the infamous Dartmouth College library rampage where blacks physically assaulted white students. The administration reacted in typical fashion by apologizing to the attackers.

In today's university, skin color matters more than shared political principles. The identity of the person behind the ideas is more important than the ideas themselves. A white person who agrees with the leftist agenda will still be marginalized because of his skin color. "They want whites to bend over backwards and make amends," says Ben Shapiro. But no matter what they do, he says, whites will "never be done paying the piper."

A new college course offering is "Whiteness Studies," designed to force white students to rub their own noses in their allegedly ingrained racism and white privilege. David Horowitz made the wry observation that black studies celebrate blackness, Chicano studies celebrate Chicanos, and whiteness studies "attack white people as evil."

THE WAR ON WHITES

Taking it even one step further is Tommy Curry, an African-American professor at Texas A&M. In his course on "Radical Black Philosophies," Curry advocates critical race theory where he says that black people should talk openly about murdering white people. The murder of whites, he says, may be necessary to achieve black liberation. He wants white people to fear blacks so much that they believe "death could come for them at any moment."

Multiculturalism creates racial division on campus where none existed previously. At Stanford, they discovered that most minority students share backgrounds that are similar to white students. During orientation, according to *The Diversity Myth* by David Sacks and Peter Thiel, minorities are forced to be different after they have been separated by the Stanford administration. It is done deliberately to justify the racist mythology that has taken over the school. The problem for the school is that there are almost no real racists at Stanford. The racial divisiveness is a farce manufactured to foment discontent.

The same applies to incidents of racism on campus. When minority students at Stanford were asked to describe concrete examples of campus racism, few were able to do so and many were bewildered by the suggestion that racism is prevalent. In order for Stanford to maintain the fiction of clear-cut racial identities, it has been necessary to manufacture evidence of cradle-to-grave oppression.

ED BRODOW

Confess Your Self-Hate

The Tucker Carlson Show reported that a school in West Bend, Wisconsin, is brainwashing adolescent children to confess that they are flawed if they happen to be white. Eighth-graders were given "a privilege test that identified them for being white or rich or having an intact family." This is common, said Tucker Carlson, in schools across the country. School officials in West Bend argued that privilege education is important to "enable the students to succeed in their careers." The officials failed to explain how shaming 12-year-old kids about their race will constitute a career booster.

"For a lot of children," said one parent, "they don't even understand what most of it means."

"If I walked up to a 13-year-old on the street and started asking these questions, I'd be put in the back of a squad car," said another parent.

Carlson challenged the idea that all people of one race are empowered and all people of another race are not. Calling the privilege test "cruel," he said it shames some kids as being "bad" for things they can't control. "How is this compassionate," Tucker asked, "to single out little kids to make them feel bad about their race or their family situation? Why would they do this to children?"

Tucker's question was answered by his guest, a liberal psychologist. It is difficult to teach history, she alleged, without talking about privilege. People must recognize what kind of privilege they have in society, she explained, "perhaps white, perhaps male." Positions of privilege "when they are abused can lead to horrible crimes committed [against] humanity."

Students must be taught to admit their privilege and not to "abuse" it as "they move forward in their lives," she continued. "Otherwise we are going to raise little boys who end up becoming producers and executives at large movie studios who end up committing crimes against women like rape."

So if 12-year-olds don't confess their privilege, they will all grow up to be sexual predators? This individual is admitting that the latest rash of sexual abuse allegations is part of the campaign to demonize all white males.

Treating Black and White Students Differently

On June 2, 2015, the *O'Reilly Factor* on *Fox News* exposed what is going on in the St. Paul, Minnesota school system, which spent millions of dollars training teachers to recognize and confront so-called white privilege. The consulting group hired by the school board recommended that teachers should treat minority students differently than whites.

According to this program, which is being instituted in many cities across the country, black students should not be disciplined for a variety of behavioral offenses because the responsibility for those behaviors lies with the white community. If a white person is assaulted by a black person, the question is: "What did the white person do to provoke that behavior?" The black assailant can be absolved of responsibility because the white person is really at fault. This is logic turned completely on its head.

Bill O'Reilly summed up the situation:

"What's happening here is that minority students at risk in poor neighborhoods are being told they don't have to obey the same rules as white kids. An underclass is being created of children who are not being held to the proper standards. The result is that those kids will leave school with a jaded view of what it takes to succeed in a competitive society. In the end, this racist educational program hurts the very children it is allegedly trying to assist. By allowing minority kids to avoid responsibility, the school districts are dooming many of them to a life of poverty and chaos."

What O'Reilly forgot to mention is that a signal is also being sent to white students: "You are racist second-class citizens who must accept responsibility for the substandard behavior of blacks."

Standardized English is Racist

The *Daily Caller* exposed another bizarre example of white bashing: "A subcommittee of an organization called the Conference on College Composition and Communication that named itself the 'Why We Cain't Breathe!' subcommittee published a list of demands calling for the abolition of 'White Mainstream English' to make way for 'Black Linguistic Justice.'" It seems that five black English professors had a tantrum because, for them, correct grammar is a ploy of white supremacists.

THE WAR ON WHITES

The group's official statement alleged that "anti-black violence toward black people in the streets across the United States mirrors the anti-black violence that is going down in these academic streets." In other words, requiring black students to use standard rules of grammar (created by whites) is just as violent as alleged street violence against blacks. That argument is one hell of a stretch, especially when you recognize that the vast majority of violence against blacks is perpetrated by other blacks, not by whites. It doesn't matter—logic has never played a large role in tantrums of any sort.

Asao Inoue, Professor of Rhetoric and Composition at Arizona State University, says it is racist to teach traditional English. "If you use a single standard to grade your students' languaging," he said, "you engage in racism. You actively promote white language supremacy, which is the handmaiden to white bias in the world. Standardized English tends to exclude many groups of people. Your students who do not embody enough of the white habits of language that make up your standards stand at your classroom doors and die for your comfort."

A well-regarded UCLA professor was disciplined for insisting that his students use the *Chicago Manual of Style*, which is de rigueur for English composition. A sit-in by a group of black students claimed it was offensive and racist. In a shameful reaction, the school's administration supported the ridiculous claims of the "offended" students. "UCLA's response to the sit-ins was a travesty of justice," Heather Mac Donald wrote in *City Journal*. "Asking for better grammar is inflammatory in the school," said an intimidated UCLA teaching assistant. "You have to give an A or you're a racist."

I will not remember Bill Cosby for his fame as an actor and comedian. Nor will I remember him for the notoriety caused by his sex scandal. I will always remember Cosby for the courage he displayed when he told the truth about language to the black community. Addressing the NAACP on the 50th anniversary of *Brown v. Board of Education*, Cosby criticized the use of African-American vernacular:

> "They're standing on the corner and they can't speak English. I can't even talk the way these people talk: Why you ain't, where you is, what he drive... And I blamed the kid until I heard the mother talk. And then I heard the father talk. Everybody knows it's important to speak English except these knuckleheads. You can't be a doctor with that kind of crap coming out of your mouth. In fact, you'll never get any kind of job making a decent living. People marched and were hit in the face with rocks to get an education, and now we've got these knuckleheads walking around."

Cosby said that African-Americans should no longer blame discrimination, segregation, governmental institutions, or white people for higher unemployment rates among blacks or the racial achievement gap. Instead, he criticized the prevalence of single-parent families and an overall lack of responsibility. He argued that blacks have their own culture of poverty and victimhood to blame. Cosby's conclusion:

THE WAR ON WHITES

"Brown or black versus the Board of Education is no longer the white person's problem. We have got to take the neighborhood back. People used to be ashamed. Today a woman has eight children with eight different 'husbands.' We have millionaire football players who cannot read. We have million-dollar basketball players who can't write two paragraphs. We, as black folks, have to do a better job. We have to start holding each other to a higher standard. We cannot blame the white people any longer."

The danger posed by attacks on English grammar and usage is that, if taken to their logical conclusion, they will lead to a demand that the pursuit of excellence is unacceptable because it is intrinsically a product of white supremacy.

Ultimately, the only way blacks can lift themselves up is to embrace the value of education. "Black educational weakness," says Shelby Steele, "has been treated primarily as a problem of racial injustice rather than as a problem of blacks rejecting or avoiding full responsibility for raising their performance levels."

Do You Want Johnnie to Be a Moron for the Rest of His Life?

Little Johnnie is an eight-year-old black student in Portland. His math teacher posed a question for the class: "How much is two plus two?" Johnnie answered: "Seven." Should the teacher do her job and correct him? Hell no, says the State of Oregon. If you correct him, it is an example of racism. It will hurt little Johnnie's feelings and he will grow up with low self-esteem. The real question—apparently ignored by the Oregon academics—is, will it hurt Johnnie's feelings to be a moron for the rest of his life?

Why is this happening to poor little Johnnie? The answer is that insane government overreach on race and gender is contaminating the American social landscape. In Johnnie's case, the Oregon Department of Education has instituted a "math equity" training for teachers so they can "dismantle racism in mathematics." Helping Johnnie find the right answer is considered a symbol of white supremacy.

Oregon's training, says *The New York Post*, encourages teachers not to give Johnnie a single correct answer, but to come up with at least two answers that might solve the problem. As far as Oregon is concerned, "The concept of mathematics being purely objective is unequivocally false." Teachers in Oregon have a responsibility to "identify and challenge the ways that math is used to uphold capitalist, imperialist, and racist views." The focus on getting the "right" answer and requiring students to "show their work" are racist, didn't you know.

"This is simply the latest in a string of 'anti-racism' teachings that insist the core of education is based on white supremacy," says Ashe Schow in *The Daily Wire*. It is also the latest in the proliferation of critical race theory, the view that the US is inherently racist, that minorities and women are oppressed by whites and especially by white men, and that white people achieve their economic and political objectives at the expense of people of color.

THE WAR ON WHITES

Biden has endorsed the racist 1619 Project, aimed at teaching school children that America was founded to enforce slavery and that its institutions continue to discriminate against black Americans. For all Biden's talk about unity, his administration has bought into identity politics and racial division. Because of it, the country is approaching a state of chaos.

Is there an end to government overreach into our private lives? The Democrats have unquestioning support from the media, academia, Big Tech, and Hollywood. Facebook and others in social media are in cahoots with the racial inquisition. Not since the McCarthy scare of the 1950s have we witnessed a situation where people can lose their ability to earn a living if they don't espouse acceptable views. "The alliance of leftists and woke capitalists hopes to regulate the innermost thoughts of every American, from school age to retirement," said Sen. Josh Hawley. "If you want to get a good job, stay at hotels and be served at restaurants, you will need to voice the right opinions. You will need to endorse the right ideas. You will need to conform."

The danger of anti-white indoctrination on campus is that, "We are cultivating students who lack all understanding of the principles of the American founding," said Heather Mac Donald. She adds:

"The students currently stewing in delusional resentments and self-pity will eventually graduate, and some will seize levels of power more far-reaching than those they currently wield over toadying campus bureaucrats and spineless faculty. What we have always

regarded as a precious inheritance could be eroded beyond recognition, and a soft totalitarianism could become the new American norm."

Teachers Unions Demand
Anti-White Discrimination

When parents began expressing their justifiable outrage at school board meetings, objecting to critical race theory being taught to their kids, teachers union leaders publicly condemned them as domestic terrorists and persuaded the Biden Justice Department to investigate them. Union leaders said that if parents don't like their children being grouped into racially based "oppressor" or "oppressed" classes, they are racist. This is just one of many indications that teachers unions have surrendered to the extreme Left.

In 2022, the Minneapolis Federation of Teachers and Minneapolis Public Schools teachers unions openly discriminated against white teachers in their new collective bargaining agreement, which specifies that teachers can be fired based solely on race. The contract states, "If excessing a teacher who is a member of a population underrepresented among licensed teachers in the site, the district shall excess the next least-senior teacher, who is not a member of an underrepresented population." In other words, white teachers should be fired before black or brown teachers, regardless of seniority.

The Minneapolis union bemoaned the lack of diversity. "What they mean," said TV commentator Allie Beth Stuckey, "is melanin count—the most superficial form of diversity.

They are only interested in how a person looks. This is the Ibram X. Kendi antiracist method of equity: past discrimination justifies present discrimination." White teachers are being punished because of their skin color and it is motivated by resentment, malice, bitterness, and anger, said Stuckey.

Fox News reported that according to the Minneapolis teachers, the clearly discriminatory guidelines are needed to resolve "past discrimination." The Minneapolis Federation of Teachers is affiliated with the National Education Association (NEA) and the American Federation of Teachers (AFT), America's two largest teachers unions.

Meanwhile in 2023, the *New York Post* reports that the New York City teachers union is sponsoring a virtual workshop on fighting back against "the harmful effects of whiteness in our lives." The workshop claims that participants will leave with a better understanding of how to center themselves as a form of resistance against whiteness. Council Minority Leader Joe Borelli, who opposed the workshop, said he was contacted by many fuming teachers and parents wondering why fighting so-called "toxic whiteness" has become a top priority for a lefty union representing a school system plagued by poor performance in the classroom.

Nine states have passed new laws pushing back against teaching anti-white critical race theory in the classroom, and similar proposals are up for consideration in more than a dozen others. School officials might deny that they're openly teaching CRT, but the nation's largest teachers union is launching a campaign to have them do just that. Delegates at the NEA's annual meeting approved a statement calling for a campaign to implement CRT in curriculum and oppose efforts to ban it. The AFT also supports CRT. AFT President Randi Weingarten said the union is preparing litigation and has a legal defense fund to fight those who attempt to limit teaching critical race theory.

"Mark my words," said Weingarten. "Our union will defend any member who gets in trouble for teaching honest history." Honest history, Ms. Weingarten, does not include CRT, an anti-white radical ideology.

"The irony of the teachers unions' deploring racism in education is glaring," says Larry Sand, president of the California Teachers Empowerment Network, "because it is the very same unions that essentially imprison children—notably poor children of color—in substandard public schools. Teachers unions are standing at the schoolhouse door fighting tooth-and nail against any kind of parental choice. The NEA, an organization that frequently rails about systemic racism, is guilty of that sin."

An Effective Way to Push Back

The medical school at the University of Oklahoma has created a diversity alliance to incorporate equity into its curriculum. This and other DEI initiatives at the university have sparked a movement to curb donations to the school. "I'm not happy with the way they're headed," said Christopher Boxell, a neurosurgeon who has been a major financial donor. "We all should be looking at who is best qualified," he said. "I don't care which race they're from. If they're best qualified, that's who should be there."

One big Oklahoma U. donor objected to DEI programs that foster racial and social division. "OU's DEI efforts produce the opposite of diversity and inclusion," she said. "Mainstream Oklahomans know they will now be labeled 'privileged' individuals regardless of life circumstances, meaning OU is not a welcoming place for all students. As a proud Oklahoman, I cannot support the deliberate destruction of our state's future. I will not donate to OU's academic efforts any longer."

A multi-million-dollar OU donor announced that he will cease his donations in response to a required class where students are taught that white people are guilty of racism. "They teach people that no matter how hard they work, white people are going to keep them down."

Carl Neuss, a seven-figure contributor to Cornell University, withheld a requested donation because of liberal indoctrination on campus. A number of professors told Neuss they felt humiliated by required diversity training. "If you say the wrong words, you could lose your position or be shunned," he said.

Hitting academia in the pocketbook may be the best way to get the message across.

Chapter Five
Anti-White Ideologies

The Left's support of anti-white policies is based on a network of ideologies, from critical race theory to Black Lives Matter. These ideologies are supported by provocative literature that bashes whites.

Critical Race Theory

The ideology behind the "all whites are racists" movement is critical race theory. One of the worst ideas ever invented by the Left, CRT wants to reintroduce racism and segregation to the forefront of American life.

Angela Onwuachi-Willig, an "expert" on CRT at Boston University School of Law, told the *Boston Globe* that, "Race and racism are basically baked into everything we do in our society. It's embedded in our institutions. It's embedded in our minds and hearts." And where does it originate? With white people, naturally. Critical race theory says if you are white, you are racist whether you realize it or not. Congratulations.

Fox's Greg Gutfeld isn't buying it. Critical race theory, says Gutfeld, redefines America as an engine of oppression. CRT has given rise to catastrophic social division that is busy destroying critical American values, including the legacy of Martin Luther King and the civil rights movement. The Left supports racism so long as it is directed at whites.

Biden has adopted this radical dogma as a pillar of his administration. He wants to abolish the fundamental American value known as meritocracy. He doesn't want us to choose the most qualified brain surgeon, airline pilot, or Marine. Equity and CRT support giving preferences to anyone who is not a straight white male. This is the ideology of the Democrat Party to which Joe Biden has surrendered.

The hypocrisy of critical race theory is that it amounts to the number one expression of outright racism since Alabama Governor George Wallace blocked the path of black students trying to enter the University of Alabama. Only this time the bigotry is aimed at white people. In the Left's perverted definition, "diversity" implies intolerance of Caucasians. Demonizing all whites as unrepentant racists is the Left's way of making white people into a minority. For the Left, the whole purpose of diversity is division. For the rest of us, "It has not been our diversity," said black economist Thomas Sowell, "but our ability to overcome the problems inherent in diversity, and to act together as Americans, that has been our strength."

Ignoring the obvious connection between black criminality and black incarceration, Democrat mayors in cities such as New York, San Francisco, and Chicago—all of whom are black—continue to blame white racism. They are using equity and CRT as a diversion from dealing with the real problem, black crime and violence, and instead claiming that the actual problem is white supremacy.

ED BRODOW

New York Mayor Eric Adams has decided to follow in the footsteps of Seattle. He is forcing all city employees into CRT-inspired training. "The training," explains a memo sent by the city, "provides all NYC employees with a framework to understand the importance of racial equity in the workplace. Become aware of systemic racism and the possible presence of racial inequality in your workplace. Understand the dominant cultural patterns of your workplace and whether they are hurting or helping your diversity, equity and inclusion goals."

In plain English, Mayor Adams is abdicating his responsibility to fight crime by pointing a finger at whites. Offering a hint of his true agenda, Adams has expressed his approval of the weak-on-crime stance of the new Manhattan district attorney, Alvin Bragg. Bragg won election "on a highly progressive platform advocating a prosecutorial focus on 'racial equity,'" Hannah E. Meyers writes in *City Journal*, "that embraces non-prosecution, minimizing detention in favor of decarceration and decriminalization."

"Adams should take crime seriously," said Meyers:

"Allowing social programs to take the place of a serious crime-fighting policy is a strategy doomed to fail. Violent crime is a terrifying preoccupation for New Yorkers, especially black ones. Blacks make up roughly one-fifth of city residents, but they are wildly overrepresented as both perpetrators and victims. Eric Adams can do something about this reality. He can continue programs that encourage rigorous paths toward productive, stable

lives, while supporting an accountable, intelligent, and well-manned police department. He can support equal opportunity by reaffirming the rule of law. And he can stand up for all New Yorkers by demonstrating that crime doesn't pay."

Instead, Adams has rejected both equal opportunity and the rule of law. His inane answer to the city's crime problem is CRT training that puts the blame on alleged white racism. I can only wonder which solution New Yorkers would prefer: (1) letting the city's white citizens know that their unconscious bias will not be tolerated by Mr. Adams, or (2) crime statistics that are finally brought under control by sensible law and order policies from the mayor's office.

To his credit, President Trump directed government agencies to purge CRT from federal employee training. "The divisive, false, and demeaning propaganda of the critical race theory movement," said Trump's OMB Director Russell Vought, "is contrary to all we stand for as Americans and should have no place in the federal government." Sadly, Trump's policy has been reversed by his successor. White government employees are once again being subjected to a racial inquisition. Biden has nominated Kiran Ahuja, an advocate of CRT, to be the director of the Office of Personnel Management. The appointment will "allow her to reinstate race-based training sessions throughout the entire federal government," said Sen. Josh Hawley.

ED BRODOW

Black Lives Matter

The emergence of Black Lives Matter was a consequence of the 2014 police shooting of Michael Brown in Ferguson, Missouri. Contrary to leftist propaganda, BLM is an anti-First Amendment gang that advocates violence, dissolution of the nuclear family, disbanding the police, and reparations for blacks.

BLM has done nothing to help black people. Its objective is the destruction of American institutions using race as a vehicle. BLM is strictly a political gift from the Left. The Left's intention is to divide the country ... and they are doing one hell of a job.

The assumption of Black Lives Matter is that blacks can claim a monopoly as objects of bigotry. Try telling that to Hispanics, Jews, Irish, Italians, Asians and other groups that have been on the receiving end of discrimination and intolerance.

John McWhorter, who happens to be black, is an American linguist and associate professor of linguistics at Columbia University. He is the author of *Woke Racism: How a New Religion Has Betrayed Black America*. McWhorter says this about BLM:

"There is a group of people who are committed to what they call social justice and they are certain enough of their moral theory that they are willing to hurt other people if they don't agree with their principles. Their notion is that they are saving people who are living under the power of the white hegemony. The problem with it is

that not only are these people mean, not only are they unpleasant to deal with, but in the name of social justice for black people, they often either don't care about black people or they are hurting black people."

If you wanted to destroy America from within, how would you do it? A good place to start would be to attack its values, especially the respect we have for the rule of law. Such an attack is taking place before our eyes. We have ceded our cities to the mob, also known as Black Lives Matter. In the wake of the George Floyd incident in 2020, the US experienced 633 violent protests in 220 cities and towns. Most of them were instigated by BLM activists.

"Black Lives Matter and their white Marxist brethren in Antifa don't want to simply demonize white America, they want to destroy it," said Jim Cegielski, publisher of *Leader-Call*. He compares BLM and Antifa to the Nazis. "Democrats, the media and large corporations better be careful of supporting the terrorist anti-American behavior of both of these groups because they will eventually turn on them."

BLM is a cover for attempted political control by the Left. It is a criminal Marxist enterprise using race as an excuse for the violent overthrow of the civil society. Based on the false narrative that cops are killing blacks, BLM places the blame for all the ills of black America on the shoulders of a so-called tradition of white racism. David Horowitz, in *I Can't Breathe*, demonstrates that Black Lives Matter has lied about every one of the twenty-six most notorious cases of police "racism" in its quest to undermine law and order and fuel race hatred.

Racism justifies everything, BLM insists, including the use of violence. "BLM believes in force," says Fox's Tucker Carlson. "They flood the streets with angry young people who break things and hurt anyone who gets in the way. Until violence stops working, violence will continue." A member of the Seattle BLM mob said, "We know that when we burn things down, we get what we want."

"I would hope by now that it is clear to everyone that the protesting, rioting, looting, vandalism and anarchy that has gripped this nation has nothing to do with ending racism," said Jim Cegielski. "Actually, it is the complete opposite. It has everything to do with promoting racism, but this time it is racism against white people. It's about the false narrative that white people are evil and must be punished for the crime of being born white."

Black author Shelby Steele explained the birth of BLM this way: "By 1968 black anger and militancy had replaced the passivism of the King era as the best means to opportunity and power for blacks. Anger in the oppressed is a response to perceived opportunity, not to injustice. Black rage is always a kind of opportunism." The non-violent approach endorsed by Martin Luther King was not producing sufficient "opportunity."

A radical subset of the black community understood that white guilt offered a more seductive prize than non-violence. White guilt is a powerful force that many believe was responsible for the election of Barack Obama. "For black leaders in the age of white guilt," Steele writes, "the problem was how to seize all they could get from white guilt without having to show actual events of racism." The solution offered by BLM was systemic racism. Its existence could be proved by the smallest racial incident. "This is why one black man being beaten by police could trigger a massive riot," Steele says. BLM launched a riot to "the scale of systemic racism rather than to the scale of the single racist event." It explains how an isolated incidence of police brutality in Minneapolis caused massive demonstrations throughout the nation and the world.

Contrary to the BLM version of reality, what happened to George Floyd was an isolated event. It does not represent how the vast majority of police treat black suspects, nor is it proof that America suffers from systemic racism. Black extremists, and especially BLM, have decided to blame whites instead of acknowledging that they themselves are at fault. The unwillingness to acknowledge Floyd's violent criminal record illustrates how blacks have avoided taking responsibility for their collective behavior.

The reaction of BLM to the Floyd case fits a pattern in which BLM exaggerates alleged injustices to blacks, says David Horowitz, "beginning with the never-documented charge of systemic racism." He goes on to say:

"Not one cop accused by Black Lives Matter can reasonably be described as having committed a cold-blooded murder, that is, a premeditated killing without extenuating circumstances. Nor can they be described as white racists determined to kill innocent blacks. By contrast, every cop killed by an individual inspired by Black Lives Matter's reckless claims was murdered in cold blood, and murdered because he was a cop and not

black. The casualties of the scorched-earth war by Black Lives Matter dwarf the total casualties of all the alleged racial injustices the organization has protested. The atrocities instigated and inspired by BLM encompass scores of innocent wounded and dead, both black and white. The crippling of police departments has led to out-of-control rates of murder and violent crime that affect, ironically and first of all, America's most vulnerable black communities."

Portraying America as "an incurable mass of bigoted whites," in the words of Ben Shapiro, has become a national pastime. But is it true? Black America, says Shelby Steele, "no longer has the excuse of oppression. Without oppression—and it must be acknowledged that blacks are no longer oppressed in America—the group itself becomes automatically responsible for its inferiority and non-competitiveness." It is much easier to avoid that responsibility "by arguing that whites should be responsible for our development. And so, once again severed from responsibility we became slaves again, our fate the responsibility of others."

Victimization plays a major role in Black Lives Matter. Steele says:

"When America acknowledged its racism, it effectively made blacks into the nation's official and, seemingly, permanent victims. It was an injustice to make victims responsible for their own problems. To do so would be to 'blame the victim,' thereby repeating his victimization.

THE WAR ON WHITES

Now I was the one—as a victim—who possessed an almost reckless moral authority. Now I could shame and silence whites at will. This power to shame, silence, and muscle concessions from the larger society on the basis of past victimization became the new 'black power.' It evolved into what we call today 'the race card.' Now America had to prove itself to me."

BLM would not be flourishing without the enthusiastic collaboration of whites. According to Rasmussen polls, an astounding 62 percent of likely voters have a favorable opinion of BLM. Millions are being donated by virtue-signaling sycophants. That seems to include Corporate America. Disney, for example, has given "full-throated support" to BLM at the same time it boycotted Fox News host Tucker Carlson because Carlson expressed deep criticism of BLM—what he called the most powerful political force in the country.

"Don't get me started on the billions of dollars of corporate money that is being thrown at this terrorist organization," said Jim Cegielski. "Apple, Amazon, Microsoft and Nike are just a few of the dozens of big corporations that are treating a domestic terrorist organization like this one as the second coming of the Boys and Girls Club of America. It's sick, it's appeasement and it's no better than those who supported the Nazi Party in 1920."

I was reluctant to believe that whites are partaking of the BLM Kool Aid until I watched a large crowd of whites on their knees confessing their racism. It is an indication of the power of white guilt. On a more personal level, a woman I have

ED BRODOW

known for 20 years, on discovering my disapproval of BLM, wrote this: "I am astonished and crushed. I thought you were better, more loving and smarter than this." Yes, I am no longer the smart, loving person she knew. To her I am a racist, irrespective of my reasons. This is how people are intimidated by the BLM agenda. "BLM now enjoys almost complete immunity from criticism," says Carlson. Saying "all lives matter" is considered hate speech. People are being fired from their jobs for uttering those simple words. In all probability, I will be struck down by lightning just for writing this book.

"Democrats," Tucker Carlson says, "believe their long-term goals align with those of BLM." In other words, the Democratic Party hopes to gain power through anarchy and the mob. We can't afford the luxury of embracing BLM violence. A civilized society cannot tolerate lawlessness. The section of Seattle that was controlled by the mob represents a phenomenon that, if not checked, will spread throughout the country like a cancer.

The law-abiding residents of black communities want an effective police force that shows zero tolerance for violent protests. These decent black citizens are the principal victims of BLM chaos, not Oprah Winfrey and other wealthy black celebrities who support BLM.

The Rise of Black Supremacy

"The biggest terror threat in this country is white men, and we have to start doing something about them," said Don Lemon when he was on *CNN*. For his daily anti-white rants,

Lemon reportedly earned $4 million per year. He is not the only TV "journalist" who hates white people. "[Kyle Rittenhouse is] being prosecuted in front of a nearly all-white jury, before a white judge in a country where white vigilantism is often excused, if not worshipped," said Joy Reid on MSNBC. "This country was built on the idea that white men have a particular kind of freedom that only they have."

Lemon and Reid typify a new breed of black TV reporters who specialize in overt racial attacks on white America, accusing it of being the number one problem facing the nation. "Joy Reid is a racist sociopath," wrote Miranda Devine in the *New York Post*. "Every night she spews hatred against white people. Shame on MSNBC for elevating such a hate-filled racist to prime time."

If white reporters made similar attacks on black America, they would be convicted of white supremacy and fired immediately. How is Reid getting away with her attacks on white America without losing her job? "For some unfathomable reason," says Devine, "she has Teflon protection at the network." That protection derives from a new element in the American social landscape, black supremacy. The acceptance of anti-white slurs made by Lemon and Reid serve as proof that black supremacy has more clout than white supremacy.

Not only do we have nonstop reporting from the media about white supremacy, even the president has complained about it. The reality is just the opposite. For at least ten years, we have been witnessing open season on white people. If white supremacy existed, this would never happen.

The tables have turned. Instead of whites being accorded special privileges as in the past, what we are witnessing now is black supremacy. African-Americans are accorded special treatment across the board. "Blackness has become a tremendous asset in contemporary America," says Ben Shapiro. "Victim status is treasured in America, and black skin guarantees automatic victim status."

Being black today, Shapiro concludes, grants privileges ranging from landing coveted college scholarships to affirmative action hiring quotas to corporate diversity training that portrays blacks in a positive light and whites negatively, and to the toleration of racist TV reporters like Lemon and Reid. It even applies to the White House, says David Horowitz, author of *Black Skin Privilege and the American Dream*. "Barack Obama was an inexperienced presidential candidate," said Horowitz, "who wouldn't be elected dogcatcher if he wasn't black."

Here are some examples of black privilege:

- Affirmative action quotas benefiting blacks have become the norm in education and employment.
- College courses are specially designed for black students.
- Black students benefit from the lower standards applied by college professors who practice affirmative grading.
- Political correctness supports anything related to African-Americans and condemns Caucasian-Americans.

- Corporate diversity programs are designed to benefit blacks.
- Many courts are reluctant to prosecute blacks for various criminal acts for fear of being called racist.
- Media bias caters to positive depictions of blacks and avoids negative ones.
- Blacks can get away with racial slurs against whites, but whites can't use the N word.

A blaring example of black supremacy can be found in today's television commercials. Blacks comprise 12 percent of the population but appear in 90 percent of commercials. It has been suggested that a person arriving from another planet would assume after watching the tube that most of the US population must be black. Diversity is one thing, but this is overcompensation driven by black supremacy.

A more insidious example of black supremacy arose after a number of Asians were assaulted in New York, San Francisco, and other cities. An attempt was made by the Left to blame the attacks on white supremacy, despite the undisputed fact that all of the reported assaults were perpetrated by blacks. One might reasonably ask, how can this be white supremacy if blacks were responsible? An answer was offered by Colorado college professor Jennifer Ho: "Anti-Asian racism has the same source as anti-black racism: white supremacy. So when a black person attacks an Asian person, the encounter is fueled perhaps by racism, but very specifically by white supremacy. White supremacy does not require a white person to perpetuate it."

Really? When a black person commits a crime, black supremacy often succeeds in relieving that person of responsibility by blaming white people who had nothing to do with it. A similar argument has been offered as proof that the Rittenhouse shootings were motivated by white supremacy, despite the fact that all of the victims were white. Biden himself called Kyle Rittenhouse a white supremacist. If whiteness were supreme, no one would dare to point a finger at Rittenhouse regardless of his motives.

So far, black supremacy has succeeded in hiding the reality of self-destructive black behaviors under the radar. "A doctrine of black supremacy," said Martin Luther King, "is as dangerous as a doctrine of white supremacy." It would be nice to get rid of both of them. How to do it is the difficult question.

The Prevalent Anti-White Literature

Two books have emerged as the leading proponents of anti-white hate: *White Fragility* and *How to be an Antiracist*. Despite being poorly written with a vile message, both of them have hit the bestseller charts. They are an insult to every unfortunate white person who has been intimidated into reading them.

The Fragility of *White Fragility*

The number one book wallowing in anti-white racism has sold a gazillion copies. It is *White Fragility: Why It's So Hard for White People to Talk About Racism* by Robin DiAngelo. The author is a former lecturer at the University of Washington who now gets paid big bucks for haranguing white audiences about their unconscious bias. She is also a racist, as this book makes patently clear from page one. DiAngelo hates everyone. She readily admits that she is very uncomfortable at the thought of having to be in the company of black people. She is white and hates white people.

White Fragility should be entitled, *The Anti-White Handbook*. The purpose of *White Fragility* seems to be making whites feel guilty about being white. As defined by DiAngelo, "white fragility" is the reluctance of white people to discuss race because we know deep down that we have unearned privilege by being white and we don't want to admit it. If you are white and don't know you are racist, or simply deny it, you are lying because all whites are racist due to their skin color, period. If a white person avoids discussing racism, DiAngelo insists they must be racist.

According to DiAngelo, when white people say, "I was taught to treat everyone the same," that is "unconvincing to people of color and invalidates their experiences. It is not possible to teach someone to treat everyone the same." If a white person says, "I treat everyone equally," they are in denial. All whites treat people of color with bigotry. Are you beginning to get a sense of the racial paranoia that runs through *White Fragility*?

When DiAngelo says that only whites can be racist, she means that in the US, only whites have "the collective social and institutional power and privilege over people of color. People of color do not have this power and privilege over white people." Therefore, people of color can't be racist.

"Individual whites may be 'against' racism, but they still benefit from a system that privileges whites as a group. Stating that racism privileges whites does not mean that individual white people do not struggle or face barriers. It does mean that we do not face the particular barriers of racism."

Here is a selection of aggravating statements from *White Fragility*:

"White supremacy is the definition of whites as the norm or standard for humanity, and people of color as a deviation from that norm."

Make America Great Again is racist, "diverting blame away from the white elite and toward various peoples of color."

"Deeply held white associations of black people with crime distort reality and the actual direction of danger that has historically existed between whites and blacks."

The more blacks in an area, the more dangerous that area is perceived to be—DiAngelo claims that actual statistics show that is not true, so she says it is a racist attitude.

"Anti-blackness is foundational to our very identities as white people."

Objection to equity is "white racial trauma."

THE WAR ON WHITES

"A positive white identity is an impossible goal."

DiAngelo relates a story about a black woman who is upset that a white woman talks over her. The black woman asks her not to do it. The white woman is upset because she says she does it with everyone, so what's the big deal? DiAngelo criticizes the white woman for not understanding that blacks are especially sensitive to whites' behavior, but she never criticizes the black woman who hasn't tried to understand the white woman's perspective. Don't blacks also have a duty to be sensitive to whites? Apparently DiAngelo doesn't think so.

The more I delved into this book, the more offended I became by the combination of the author's authoritarian prose together with her obvious hatred of both white and black people. After reading the entire 150 pages of this nonsense, I have the feeling that DiAngelo believes anything I say or do in front of people of color will be interpreted as racist, so my best course of action is either to keep my mouth shut, avoid people of color entirely, or spend most of my time apologizing to blacks. When Ms. DiAngelo reads my review of her book, she will undoubtedly attribute most of it to my unconscious racism. It is very difficult if not impossible to win an argument with someone as omniscient as she is.

A Latina friend of mine was offended by DiAngelo's use of the term *people of color*. "What she wrote in her book does not apply to me," said my friend, "even though I am a person of color. If she wants to talk about black people, she should say so. I don't want to be included."

My principal criticism of *White Fragility* is that nowhere does she say that blacks bear any responsibility for their lives. Everything is the fault of white people who refuse to acknowledge their racism. DiAngelo, in effect, is claiming that blacks lack the capacity to make their own decisions. They are powerless victims of oppressive white people. She does a disservice to black people by perpetuating their entanglement in victimhood.

Similarly, DiAngelo never acknowledges the possibility that blacks do some things that might be offensive to whites. She seems to ignore crime and violence when perpetrated by black people. If whites have the nerve to bring it up, it means they are racist.

Now that you know what I think, here are some other reviews:

"Systemic racism of the kind espoused by DiAngelo places the problems of blacks onto the shoulders of whites and negates the agency of African-Americans to improve their lot," says Scott Greer. "'You cannot succeed in a white supremacist nation when you're black' is the intended message of this rhetoric."

Black linguist John McWhorter, writing in *The Atlantic*, said, "*White Fragility* is truly horrific. What would all of this do for poor black people who actually need help? You can tell she doesn't give a good goddam, and when asked what she thinks of black people who don't agree with her, she basically calls us Uncle Toms." The book "openly infantilizes black people" and "simply dehumanizes us. It is racist." McWhorter goes on to say:

"I have learned that one of America's favorite advice books of the moment is actually a racist tract. Despite the sincere intentions of its author, the book diminishes black people in the name of dignifying us. This is unintentional, of course, like the racism DiAngelo sees in all whites. I'm saying that if you write a book that teaches that black people's feelings must be stepped around to an exquisitely sensitive degree that hasn't been required of any human beings, you're condescending to black people. In supposing that black people have no resilience, you are saying that black people are unusually weak. You're saying that we are lesser. You're saying that we, because of the circumstances of American social history, cannot be treated as adults."

During a webinar on racial justice, DiAngelo said: "People of color need to get away from white people." Her racially-charged comments enraged conservatives on *Twitter*. "Robin DiAngelo sounding like an old-line segregationist," anti-CRT expert Christopher Rufo tweeted in response to the webinar. Conservative podcast host Allie Beth Stuckey said DiAngelo's comments sounded like racial comments made by Dilbert creator, Scott Adams, that caused several newspapers to pull his long-running cartoon. Adams said that white people should stay away from blacks. "When Robin DiAngelo says it, it's inspirational and she gets paid $20k," Stuckey tweeted. "When Scott Adams says it, it's racist and he loses his job."

ED BRODOW

I will close with this anonymous review from *Amazon*: *"It is a popular book for those that need more of a reason to feel bad about themselves."*

Anti-White Ravings of an Antiracist

The second hot book that is guilty of anti-white racism is the racist *How to Be an Antiracist* by Ibram X. Kendi. When I slogged through *White Fragility*, I thought it was one of the worst books I'd ever read. Then I read Kendi's book and by comparison, DiAngelo's book is right up there with Tolstoy. *Antiracist* is very difficult to read. Kendi rambles so much that most of the time, I had no idea what the hell he was talking about. Sorry, but 238 pages of his drivel is 237 too many. I'm laughing as I think about it.

Much of *Antiracist* seemed like awkward stream of consciousness without any logical cohesion. "To be racist is ... to be an antiracist is ..." and on and on, page after page, with numerous definitions of racism that make no sense.

Most of the book consists of a series of uninteresting stories recounting Kendi's childhood and adolescence in New York City and Philadelphia. I learned nothing of value about the race issue other than Kendi is angry at being a black man in a white society. Kendi evidently doesn't like white people any more than Robin DiAngelo. "To be American," he says, "is to be white." That is not meant as a compliment.

Kendi objects that blacks have to conform to white society. His objection would be justified if white society was awful, e.g., Nazi Germany. But whites have created a laudable society that has much to offer blacks and anyone else who is fortunate enough to live in the US. Kendi never tells us what blacks have to offer that is better.

Kendi also bemoans his observation that blacks can't be themselves in a group of white people. What he really is saying is that blacks should not be tolerant of white behaviors. As a white man, if I am in a group of blacks or Hispanics or Asians, I can still be myself while enjoying the differences. I don't dislike them because they are different. Their being different does not take anything away from me. Kendi thinks he is diminished when in the presence of whites. This clearly illustrates Kendi's anti-white hatred.

One of *Antiracist*'s many definitions of racism is that discrimination creates inequity. Kendi is disturbed that a greater percentage of whites than blacks live in their own homes. That is inequitable. "An example of racial equity," he says, "would be if there were relatively equitable percentages of all three racial groups [white, black, "Latinx"] living in owner-occupied homes."

His solution, and the main thrust of Kendi's philosophy, is this: *"The only remedy to racist discrimination is antiracist discrimination. The only remedy to past discrimination is present discrimination. The only remedy to present discrimination is future discrimination."*

Translation: Kendi believes in an extreme form of affirmative action—discriminating against whites in order to bring blacks up to par. He thinks Dr. King's dream of a color-blind society is racist. Kendi is advocating equity over equality, so I am certain he approves of Biden's executive order on equity.

Kendi's attitude about black violence is disturbing. After insisting that blacks are not as violent as whites think they are, he describes a group of black teenagers viciously beating up an Asian boy for sitting in the wrong part of a bus. Then he says he wants to "flee misbehaving black folk." Yet he was offended when President Reagan supported anti-crime measures. "His 'stronger law enforcement' sent more black people into the clutches of violent cops, who killed twenty-two black people for every white person." If you can make sense out of that sentence, you must be smarter than I am.

Another statement makes little sense: Kendi claims that climate is racist because the non-white South is being victimized by climate change more than the whiter North. Help!

John McWhorter thought *Antiracist* was utterly worthless. "If you're not being actively anti-racist, then you qualify as racist. I don't even know what that means," McWhorter says. "He's the kind of black person who grew up thinking of white people as devils. *Antiracism* treats black people like simpletons. To frame yourself as an eternal victim gives you a sense of belonging, a sense of significance, it feels good. The black American race is encouraged to O.D. on that."

Lynn Uzzell, in *RealClearPolitics*, compares Kendi with George Orwell. "The dystopian powers in '1984' deliberately turned the meaning of words upside-down in a process known as double-think. The same process is happening today as Ibram X. Kendi insists that the only way to fight racism is to embrace racial discrimination in perpetuity. This 'anti-racism,' as he calls it, is as likely to stamp out genuine racism as Orwell's Ministry of Truth was apt to stamp out falsehoods."

Let me close with two reviews from *Amazon*:

"How this witless dross made it to the New York Times *bestseller list is not a mystery. It's a sign of the times. As a culture, I sincerely hope we can overcome the mind-numbing groupthink that continues to enable this kind of wishy-washy mentality."*

"The author is a 'diarrhea of words with a constipation of ideas.' If you try to read his book, have a mountain of toilet paper available for your use."

I heartily concur. It was necessary for me to read *Fragility* and *Antiracist* as part of my research for this book. You are lucky if you don't have to. The big takeaways from both of these vicious works are: (a) the extent to which they encourage whites to hate themselves, and (b) how much they contribute to the hatred of white people by people of color. It is a tragedy that the innocent minds of our children are being poisoned because their schools force them to read this crap.

Coates' Anti-White Ravings

We need to mention Ta-Nehisi Coates, who wrote an angry book entitled, *Between the World and Me*. Coates' America is a place where blacks are threatened and violated every day. He doesn't think that the nastiness of white supremacy will ever be rooted out. "To a black reader," says Scott Greer, "his words are an incitement to despise America and the whites who supposedly control it. To white liberals, the black writer's words are gospel, and his imprecations against the past sins of whites are catnip to their guilt-laden consciences."

"Coate's ideas fit nicely into the victimhood culture," says Greer, "where whites are presented as morally inferior due to their privilege, and blacks are morally superior due to their oppression."

Coates is famous for his 2014 article that appeared in *The Atlantic*, "The Case for Reparations." He describes horrible atrocities that were perpetrated against blacks. While he admits that conditions have improved, he argues that:

> *"African-Americans still remained—by far—the most segregated ethnic group in the country. Having been enslaved for 250 years, black people were not left to their own devices. They were terrorized. In the Deep South, a second slavery ruled. In the North, legislatures, mayors, civic associations, banks, and citizens all colluded to pin black people into ghettos, where they were overcrowded, overcharged, and undereducated. Businesses discriminated against them, awarding them the worst jobs and the worst wages. Police brutalized them in the streets. And the notion that black lives, black bodies, and black wealth were rightful targets remained deeply rooted in the broader society."*

THE WAR ON WHITES

Out of this analysis, Coates makes a case for reparations. "What I'm talking about is more than recompense for past injustices—more than a handout, a payoff, hush money, or a reluctant bribe. What I'm talking about is a national reckoning that would lead to spiritual renewal." He tries to compare reparations for blacks to German reparations made to Jews for the Holocaust, ignoring the fact that the latter is still fresh in people's lives and minds while slavery is ancient history. No one alive today was a slave or a slave owner. (See my discussion of reparations in Chapter Seven.)

Chapter Six
Biden's Anti-White Presidency

Joseph Robinette Biden, Jr., ran on a platform of unifying the country. Instead, he has done everything in his power to foment division based on race and political affiliation.

Biden has a history full of racist statements and behaviors. During his tenure in the Senate, he praised colleagues who supported segregation. People like Virginia Senator Robert A. Byrd, former Ku Klux Klan bigshot. Biden's remarks included this bombshell about Barack Obama: "I mean, you got the first mainstream African American who is articulate and bright and clean and a nice-looking guy. I mean, that's a storybook, man." His record in the Senate included opposing busing, opposing school integration, and strong friendships with racist southern senators.

With his latest executive order on equity, he is reinventing himself as a far-left proponent of radical racial policies. He is still a racist, only now his racism is aimed at white people. He tried to make it sound reasonable. "Members of underserved communities," he said, "many of whom have endured generations of discrimination and disinvestment—still confront significant barriers to realizing the full promise of our great Nation, and the Federal Government has a responsibility to remove these barriers."

THE WAR ON WHITES

Samantha Chang, writing in *The Western Journal*, is concerned that Biden's rhetoric masks his anti-white racism:

"As concerned parents nationwide protest the insidious encroachment of critical race theory into their children's classrooms, Congress quietly passed a $1.2 trillion infrastructure bill that incorporates CRT's anti-white racism into multiple taxpayer-funded programs. Why? It's because President Joe Biden's 'infrastructure' legislation made explicit provisions requiring that federal contracts be awarded using affirmative-action policies that prioritize a candidate's skin color over his or her qualifications. The president and his party are opportunistically using America's roads, subways and bridges as vehicles for 'racial justice' in a massive taxpayer-funded spending bill that marginalizes white people and prioritizes minorities. This anti-white discrimination isn't surprising, because it's a pattern with this administration. Demonizing white people and disempowering black people by encouraging them to view themselves as 'oppressed victims' will only result in more racial division and societal chaos."

At a time when many states are acting to ban racist CRT, Biden is inflicting it on the federal government. From the start of his presidency, Joe promised to make racial justice a major priority. His policies may be considered just by some identity groups, but whites are not likely to be one of them. Under the cover of combatting racism, the Biden administration is going full steam ahead with plans that can only be described as anti-white. "Biden's equity agenda," says Ray Arora in *City Journal*, "is systemic racism in disguise."

"There has been a recent trend toward the government excluding white people," says Evan Gerstmann in *Forbes Magazine*. "These exclusions go well beyond traditional affirmative action plans. While this has been occurring at the state and local level, the Biden Administration has pursued this new approach most doggedly, across a broad array of relief funds, with billions of dollars being marked as off-limits to white business owners and farmers regardless of need."

Biden's Big Push for Equity

President Biden's woke executive order 14091—*Further Advancing Racial Equity and Support for Underserved Communities Through the Federal Government*—gives the green light to extensive government enforcement of equity, critical race theory, and affirmative action.

Order 14091 requires that every federal agency must have an equity team to coordinate the implementation of Biden's racist policies. Each federal agency will be required to produce public equity action plans every year to "assess and include actions to address the barriers underserved communities may face in accessing and benefitting from the agency's policies, programs, and activities."

The equity teams will report to an equity czar who will ensure that all new federal employees will be selected based upon their skin color so that preference can be given to non-whites.

THE WAR ON WHITES

This is now the official policy of the US government. You thought America's standard was equality of opportunity? Equal treatment under the law? You were mistaken. Biden is erasing the gains from the civil rights movement by establishing race and gender criteria that are expressly prohibited by the Civil Rights Act of 1964 and the 14th Amendment. The latter requires equal protection under the law. Equity requires treating people unequally in order to achieve equal outcomes.

It is impossible to legislate equality of outcome. Biden doesn't agree. He is trying to accord special privileges to certain groups and not to one specific group—whites. He wants to do this with every department and agency of the federal government.

"Most terrifying for ordinary Americans," former Acting Assistant Attorney General Katie Sullivan writes at *amac.us*, "federal agencies have hired legions of woke bureaucrats in order to enforce this new equity agenda. Every federal agency now has a designated 'environmental justice officer' and a 'special coordinator' to work with Biden's 'Gender Policy Council.' Biden's order explicitly elevates 'advancing equity' above the traditional missions of federal agencies— namely, serving taxpayers."

The extent of Biden's order is massive, restructuring all of American society along lines of equity instead of equality. If one minority group is underperforming, Biden assumes they are "underserved." Any inequality, he believes, must be the result of bad policy instead of bad behavioral choices.

As described by *The Center for Individual Rights*, "The order furthers the administration's effort to 'embed equity into all aspects of Federal decision-making.' Racial equity is a progressive euphemism for racial reparations and preferences in education, hiring, and contracting. Biden is pushing to make the federal government a frank instrument of a racialized radicalism."

In addition to violating federal civil rights laws, Biden's equity plans "are at war with the nation's very ideals and laws," says *The Heritage Foundation*. By treating people differently based not on need, but on race or on a predetermined victimhood status, we could easily witness "a new form of political patronage and corruption through a racial spoils system."

Given Biden's stated effort to employ equity to combat what he claims is the most lethal threat to the homeland—white supremacy, said Ben Weingarten in *Newsweek*, "critical race theory would become our domestic counterterrorism policy. This administration casts critics of its policies as racists and bigots—potentially dangerous ones, insurrectionists. Domestic equity would demand pursuing non-progressives like foes of the regime."

"Worried that using race to identify and help disadvantaged communities could trigger legal challenges that would stymie their efforts," Lisa Friedman wrote in the *New York Times*, "administration officials said they were designing a system to help communities of color without defining them as such." They do this by using words such as *underserved, marginalized,* and *disadvantaged*—code words for non-white. The result is likely to be racial and sexual quotas that reward identity characteristics over merit. As an example of how the plans will favor non-white groups, *The*

THE WAR ON WHITES

Heritage Foundation suggests that "a federal agency would give priority to a wealthy Chilean-born neurologist or to a gay dentist over a poor Italian American factory worker who has fewer resources."

David Horowitz has called the application of words such as underserved and marginalized a monstrous lie. "The federal government," he said, "has provided nearly $30 *trillion* in welfare payments and other poverty handouts in the last fifty-odd years, of which all poor blacks have been legitimate recipients, along with members of other racial groups."

How Equity Plans Will Operate

Equity-based programs are likely to make the government much less efficient by giving jobs to unqualified employees, awarding contracts to uncompetitive bidders, impairing national defense, and lowering standards of excellence in the nation's schools.

The Heritage Foundation describes how various agencies will use Biden's equity plans. The Labor Department may steer favored groups into apprenticeships and federal employment. The Agriculture Department plans to increase diversity trainings. The Environmental Protection Agency plans to lower scientific standards in order to appease activist groups. Even the State Department will be swallowed up by equity requirements that will affect foreign policy and foreign assistance. The Department of Health and Human Services plans "equity assessments" that will affect how people are hired and how welfare programs are administered. The Department of Homeland Security will undoubtedly attempt to justify Biden's open border policy by focusing on equity instead of dealing with the real problems of Mexican cartels, trafficking, smuggling, and the threat of terrorism.

Hopefully the Republican-controlled House will put the brakes on Biden's overreach by limiting funding for executive orders, conducting oversight, and riding shotgun over violations of civil rights laws.

In an article entitled, "Joe Biden turns the American government into Wokeness, Inc.," Ben Shapiro emphasizes the illegality of Biden's executive order:

"Nothing gives the president of the United States the unilateral authority to reshape the entire executive branch into an agent of 'equity.' That is a legislative function, and the legislature has given no such grant of power. But Biden is doing it anyway. And that means stacking—presumably for generations to come—a Deep State of equity-driven Left-wing bureaucrats throughout the federal government. This is dangerous, and it must be stopped. It is violative of constitutional principles, both in terms of separation of powers and under the equal protection clause. The executive order is one of the broadest, most transformative executive orders in modern American history; it turns the federal government into one giant machine designed for the propagation of woke principles. The executive order set out the key guiding principle for the Biden administration. This principle, 'equity,' will now be used

*to redirect the entirety of the federal government's
awesome powers."*

Tucker Carlson described Biden's policy initiative as, "The
largest racial tracking bureaucracy since the fall of Nazi
Germany. Biden restructured the entire executive branch of
the US government to discriminate on the basis of immutable
characteristics. Joe Biden institutes a government-wide
system of racial discrimination that dwarfs Jim Crow," Tucker
said, "and nobody seems to notice."

Betsy McCaughey, former lieutenant governor of New
York, railed against Joe Biden's anti-white agenda in the *New
York Post*:

*"Unless you're a person of color or a favored minority,
brace yourself to be treated unfairly by the Biden
administration. Biden's push for equity will foment racial
hostility not seen in half a century. He's imposing anti-
white discrimination on everything, from housing to
health care. It's racism by another name. Racial equity
means government will treat people unequally,
discriminating against whites to equalize outcomes.
Older people who are white will find it harder to get an
appointment with a doctor who takes Medicare. The
Biden administration is forcing physicians to categorize
their patients by race and demonstrate they have an
'anti-racism' plan to combat health disparities. To meet
that test, black patients will be in demand; white ones not
so much. If you're white, good luck dealing with the costs
of buying a home. Fannie Mae's new Equitable Housing*

Finance Plan will help with appraisals and closing costs—but only if you're black. If you're a white company owner who sells to the federal government, get ready to lose business to a competitor who identifies as 'underserved,' 'marginalized' or 'disadvantaged'—all euphemisms for identity groups. The Biden bureaucracy gives preference to minorities in federal procurement. Straight white men can take a hike."

Despite Biden's rhetoric of 'equity for all,' wrote Caitlin Doornbos in the *New York Post,* his plan focuses exclusively on racial minorities—"from prioritizing persons of color when doling out grants and government contracts to focusing outreach efforts *specifically on non-white groups.*"

"By forcibly guaranteeing equality of outcome instead of equality of opportunity for Americans," Shawn Fleetwood wrote in *The Federalist,* "President Joe Biden tacitly admitted his administration is collaborating with a prominent leftist group to advance neo-Marxism throughout the US government." The leftist group Fleetwood is referring to is the "Justice40 Initiative," described as an attempt to "advance neo-Marxist policies under the guise of 'environmental justice.'"

"Equity is a term regularly employed by leftists to cover up their true goal of dismissing merit and real equality in favor of discrimination on the basis of skin color," Fleetwood explains. Discrimination against whites, that is. "In other words," Fleetwood concludes, "the administration is distributing taxpayer money to certain jurisdictions based on racial demographics."

THE WAR ON WHITES

Biden's equity plan will fail because affirmative action means lowering standards. Federal agencies will be forced to lower standards in order to hire unqualified applicants and the quality of our government will sink even lower than it is now. "Our government should be in the business of enabling opportunity for all," says Scott Greer, "not in picking winners. It can do so by ensuring that artificial distinctions such as race do not determine outcomes."

Writing for *The Heritage Foundation*, Mike Gonzalez said that "Biden's embrace of equity means he's abandoned the quest for equality." The executive order "requires all federal agencies to ferret out any policy that may produce unequal outcomes among ' members of categories deemed marginalized. This will put the divisive doctrine of *disparate impact* on steroids. The doctrine rests on the dubious concept that if an impartially applied policy leads to unequal outcomes, it is illegal, no matter how nondiscriminatory in intent. Policymakers will then search for racial results, and their policies will be unfair and wasteful." EO 14091 includes what Gonzalez calls "every victim category under the sun." *It excludes only one group—whites.*

"It's as if Biden has made the 'anti-racist' writer Ibram X. Kendi the head of his Office of Personnel Management," says *Minot Daily News*. "All of this is insidious. Anyone who is not on board will be intimidated into staying silent, or simply leave for another job. Obviously, some of the departments and agencies involved are enormously powerful, and their working shouldn't be skewed by ideology. Is the Department of Justice, for instance, supposed to try to adjust the FBI's arrests to achieve greater demographic balance?"

That is an interesting basis for speculation. Will the DOJ decide to establish racial quotas for federal prosecutions, *requiring a greater number of white defendants?* This is not merely a hypothetical question. Alan Dershowitz has reported that in Canada, judges have been explicitly advised that they must consider race when meting out justice. If a criminal defendant is black, that person automatically gets a reduced sentence just because they are black.

The US could be heading in the same direction. California has passed a Racial Justice Act that enables anyone to challenge a criminal conviction on the grounds of racial bias. We could easily move from there to racial quotas both for convictions and prison inmates, increasing the proportion of whites and decreasing the proportion of blacks.

Dershowitz is adamant that we should not have race-based affirmative action in criminal sentencing. The major victims of such a policy, he says, would be black people because the vast majority of crimes committed by blacks are against other blacks. If criminals benefiting from reduced sentences went out and committed more crimes against blacks, that is not a gain for the black community. "You're taking it out on innocent black victims of crime," said Dershowitz. If Biden tries to enforce his concept of equity on the justice system, the number of black crime victims will automatically be increased.

Orange Man to the Rescue

"This [executive order] matches with how Biden has run his administration," writes Zachary Faria in the *Washington*

Examiner, "constantly seeking out racist and sexist policies that benefit the groups upon which Democrats want to confer privilege. Biden has sought to impose racial and gender quotas. He's used his Cabinet not to assemble competent managers but to fill out his diversity collection, with tragic results. Biden views the world through the lens of skin color and gender only, and he is now instructing federal agencies to do the same. Biden is dragging the country backward, encouraging racial divisions and divisions along gendered lines."

Donald Trump is just the man to stop it. He promises to do exactly that if he is elected in 2024. In a recent video posted to *Truth Social,* he said:

"Every institution in America is under attack from this Marxist concept of equity. Freedom and equality under the law are absolutely dead. Equity has become a catch-all phrase for the Radical Left to justify every one of their crazy programs. Instead of treating everyone equally, making decisions based on merit or qualifications, equity means that benefits are awarded and policies are enforced based on skin color and sexual identity. Any such discrimination is totally illegal. I will immediately terminate all staffers hired to implement this policy and eliminate all offices and initiatives connected to it. We will not allow it to happen. I will create a special team to rapidly review every action taken by federal agencies under Biden's equity agenda that will need to be reversed. We will reverse all of them. I will urge Congress to create a restitution fund for Americans who have been

unjustly discriminated by this equity policy and I will restore merit based civil service. I will get this extremism out of the White House, out of the military, out of the Justice Department, and out of our government."

Perhaps a kinder way of looking at Biden's woke policies is to understand that, in the words of Shelby Steele, "In the age of white guilt, whites support all manner of silly racial policies without seeing that their true motivation is simply to show themselves innocent of racism." Calling Biden's policies "silly" understates how misguided and dangerous they are.

Chapter Seven
How the War on Whites Hurts Black People

White people are not the only ones who are being harmed by the war on whites. People of color are suffering too.

The Victim Mentality

When you demand little from a person, little is what you get. As a consequence of expecting less from black people, many African-Americans have acquired what I call a *victim mentality*: the unwillingness to take responsibility for one's own behavior and instead blaming others for life's problems. The welfare system is an outgrowth of anti-white thinking. It has imposed the victim mentality on black people, encouraging them to believe that they are oppressed by whites. As described by one web-based journal, "a violent dependency state has been created within the black community that threatens to tear America apart at the seams."

Critical race theory is based on the assumption that blacks are victims and whites are oppressors. "The litmus test for being black," said Shelby Steele, "required one to accept racial victimization not as an occasional event in one's life but as an ongoing identity." This idea has been around for a long time, and is the basis for the welfare system. Washington's foray into the social welfare business has been a disaster. The Democratic Party wants to restructure society, eliminate poverty, and improve the lives of African-Americans by giving away money and making blacks dependent on government.

We used to consider self-reliance as one of the keystones that define America. Remember the "rugged individual?" Then something unexpected happened: the Great Depression. The Roosevelt administration's New Deal attempted to transform the federal government from a modest bureaucracy into a leviathan based on progressive ideas. "Throughout the nation men and women look to us," said President Franklin Delano Roosevelt, "for more equitable opportunity to share in the distribution of national wealth." Sound familiar?

Lyndon Johnson's Great Society and War on Poverty boosted Washington's reach into the lives of everyday citizens. These invasive government programs marked the expansion of the welfare state. Thanks to the myth of the rugged individual, poverty used to be regarded as a temporary condition. Nowadays you have to look pretty hard to find rugged individuals. In their place, we have a culture of dependency. "The remarkable growth of the entitlement state," said Nicholas Eberstadt in *Foreign Affairs*, "has radically transformed both the American government and the American way of life itself.

THE WAR ON WHITES

I love this quote from Thomas Sowell: "The welfare state is the oldest con game in the world. First you take people's money away quietly and then you give some of it back to them flamboyantly. The Left's agenda is a disservice to [blacks and poor people] as well as to society."

"When America acknowledged its racism," said Shelby Steele, "it effectively made blacks into the nation's official and, seemingly, permanent victims—citizen-victims, as it were, for whom demands of responsibility are verboten lest the larger nation seem to be oppressing them all over again." Steele cites a talk by Lyndon Johnson that was "a classic white-guilt speech, implying that racial inequities are overcome solely by the efforts of whites and American institutions. The speech insistently and conspicuously refused to imagine blacks outside a framework of victimization. And no president since Johnson has done any better. It is nothing less than stunning that in the four decades of racial reform since the sixties, and amid constant racial debate, there has not been a single articulation by an American president of how blacks might so much as even share responsibility for their own advancement."

An astonishing video made the rounds on the Internet in which an unmarried African-American mother of 15 children from three different fathers exclaimed, "Somebody needs to pay for all my children. Somebody needs to be held accountable and they need to pay!" It never crossed her mind that she was responsible for having this battalion of offspring. It was as if someone had opened the roof to her house and dropped in 15 kids. She simply assumed that the state was responsible and the state would pay.

An appropriate question is: Why have Asian immigrants assimilated into the economy but blacks have not? Answer: The victim mentality among black Americans has given rise to the Victimization Industry, spearheaded by black "leaders" like Jesse Jackson and Al Sharpton. Bill O'Reilly refers to it as the "grievance industry." There is big money in keeping blacks poor and dumb. If the victim mentality were replaced by a culture of taking responsibility, people like Jackson and Sharpton would be out of business.

The victim mentality and consequent violent acting out by African-Americans is traceable to the anti-white ideology that blames white people for the condition of American blacks. So long as whites are excoriated for their alleged racist behavior, blacks will continue to suffer.

There is a way out. We can end the poverty crisis in black America if we accept two conclusions:

1. Government must stop treating black people like sub-humans who cannot function without public assistance and lowered standards. That means replacing the "give them free stuff" welfare system with programs that prepare low-income blacks for self-sufficiency. Diversity trainings and the proliferation of books like *White Fragility* prevent this from happening by focusing instead on the anti-white notions of equity and CRT.

2. African-Americans must stop blaming white people and assume responsibility for solving the problems of their own community. This is the recommendation of

many blacks including Thomas Sowell and Bill Cosby. If blacks are free, says Shelby Steele, they can't blame white people for their shortcomings. You are responsible for your own fate. Blacks decided to blame whites instead of accepting their freedom by assuming responsibility. They gave their power away.

If everyone is vying to be the top victim and the most oppressed by white people, says Scott Greer, racial discord will become ingrained in American life with "white identity being the only kind not welcome in polite society."

Reparations for Blacks—An Insupportable Idea

The notion of awarding reparations to blacks to compensate for slavery has been floating around for years without anyone taking it seriously. The idea of reparations is predicated on the anti-white canard that contemporary whites are responsible for the social and economic condition of blacks, which I have attempted to refute throughout this book.

In 2014, the argument for reparations was given a boost by an influential article that appeared in *The Atlantic*, "The Case for Reparations" by Te-Nehisi Coates. Coates himself admitted that he didn't expect it would come to fruition. "My notion wasn't that you could actually get reparations passed," said Coates, "even in my lifetime." Thanks to the racial hurricane set off by the George Floyd incident, Coates' idea has been given a new round of support.

Sen. Cory Booker and Rep. Sheila Jackson Lee proposed legislation to establish a commission for the study of reparations. The US Conference of Mayors came out in support of the bill. Evanston, Illinois, became the first US city to fund reparations.

The State of California is contemplating a cash award of $360,000 to each black resident, which would undoubtedly lead to a flood of black people from all over the country into California. Not to be outdone, an advisory committee in San Francisco has recommended $5 million payouts to black individuals, as well as guaranteed annual income of $97,000 for 250 years and personal debt forgiveness. It should be noted that the reparations task force in San Francisco was comprised mainly of blacks who have generously voted monetary payments for themselves. It is reminiscent of the anonymous quote, "A democracy can only exist until the voters discover that they can vote themselves largesse from the public treasury."

The two main reasons behind renewed interest in reparations are a resurgence of white guilt and resulting black opportunism. "Whites are hungry for a way to prove that they're innocent of racism," says Shelby Steele, so they offer "to make reparations to African-Americans and other minorities." Meanwhile black anger and militancy have become "the best means to opportunity and power for blacks. Anger in the oppressed is a response to perceived opportunity, not to injustice," Steele says. "Black rage is always a kind of opportunism." The opportunity is presenting itself now in the form of white guilt. Black opportunists like Booker and Lee are eager to take advantage of it.

THE WAR ON WHITES

Here are five reasons why reparations are insupportable:

(1) They are unfair to non-blacks who never owned slaves.

(2) Reparations are totally impractical from a fiscal viewpoint—they would bankrupt the nation for centuries.

(3) They would inflame racial discord.

(4) They would result in a taxpayer revolt.

(5) Instead of solving the problems affecting the black community, reparations would cause serious harm.

First, asking all non-blacks to fund reparations is patently unfair. Political commentator Michael Medved observed that since so many of today's Americans are descendants of post-Civil War immigrants, as few as five percent of today's whites have a "generational" connection to slavery. What gives anyone the right to demand reparations from them?

"How can all Americans in the 21st century be held financially responsible for the actions of a subset of Americans hundreds of years ago?" said Armstrong Williams in *The Hill.* "The concept makes no sense from start to finish." The same applies to non-black Americans who are people of color but have no connection to the slave system. And what about the Irish, European Jews, Hispanics, and Chinese, all of whom were subjected to severe discrimination. Should they pay reparations, or receive them?

Ying Ma, writing at *foxnews.com*, said:

"Under the logic of the current reparations proposals, descendants of early Chinese immigrants to the Golden State, like myself, should be eligible for reparations as well. That we are not even included in the discussion demonstrates the absurdity of the reparations movement. That reparations are discussed seriously at all further shows the perils of policymaking based on racial grievance and virtue signaling. It would be immoral, on the deepest level, to force Californians who bear no responsibility whatsoever for the actions of their ancestors, to pay tax dollars to their fellow residents whose ancestors suffered. Let us never force one group of people to pay off another group of people to atone for the sins of others. Let us not obsess over grievances of the past but strive, today, to treat each other equally, regardless of race, ethnicity, color or country of origin."

"The reparations argument is based on the unfounded claim that all African-American descendants of slaves suffer from the economic consequences of slavery and discrimination," says author David Horowitz. "No evidence-based attempt has been made to prove that living individuals have been adversely affected by a slave system that was ended over 150 years ago."

"Black Americans' upward mobility from Reconstruction to the present is a testament to their creativity and ability to adapt," said Stefan Spath at the *Foundation for Economic Education*. "Reparations are not only unnecessary as a financial corrective, but they would also be an insult to the multitudes of successful black Americans who lifted themselves out of poverty before and after the civil rights movement."

"Maybe I live in a box, but I've never met a single black American who was a slave or a single white American who was a slaveowner," said black activist Candice Owens. "I've only come across lazy people who believe that those of us who work ought to support them."

Slavery in America falls under the heading of ancient history. "Why are we penalizing people for what their ancestors did?" asked former NFL running back Herschel Walker. "Reparations are complicated, contentious and messy," Stuart E. Eizenstat wrote in *Politico Magazine*, "and work best when the crime was recent and the direct victims are still alive."

"White people are being called to pay for the sins of people who shared our same melanin count hundreds of years ago," said Allie Beth Stuckey. "The assumption is that all of our ancestors owned slaves. No, most of our ancestors did not own slaves. A very small percentage of Americans ever owned slaves. We're being told that black people should receive reparations because people that looked like them a long time ago endured oppression. It is based on maxims and dogma rather than truth."

Reparation hustlers offer a lame refutation: Although most living whites lack a direct connection to slaveowners, they do not have a right to unearned white privilege that exists to the detriment of black citizens. The beautiful home that you own in a safe, white neighborhood; the substantial income you receive; the investments you have made that give you economic security; the legal advantages that accrue to you; the societal power that all whites enjoy—all of these advantages are yours at the expense of black suffering. It is only fair and equitable for you to share those advantages with the black population that continues to be deprived of such a legacy. Reparations presumably would atone for that racist inequality. Sorry, Charlie, I am not buying it. It is neither fair nor equitable to make demands based on ancient history.

Second, paying reparations is impractical. From a fiscal standpoint, it is totally irresponsible. A study by three college professors puts the price tag of the Booker-Lee proposal at $6.2 quadrillion. The US would be bankrupt for five centuries.

From an enforcement perspective, how would it be determined who should receive benefits and who should pay? "Because of centuries of migration, conquests, and intermixing, racial purity is more of a social construct than a biological fact," said Stefan Spath. "Intermarriage between whites and blacks in America over the past two centuries has produced a large population of individuals who defy the stark dichotomy. With so much racial intermixture, will those who dole out the potential reparations demand certificates of racial purity? The thought is preposterous." Black talk show host Larry Elder pointed to mixed-race Democrats including Kamala Harris and Barack Obama, asking, "Do [they] pay a check or receive a check?"

Third, reparations would cause racial discord. The backlash from a program of reparations would generate societal collapse. "Rather than promote the reconciliation we so badly need," said Stuart Eizenstat, "reparations could seriously inflame racial tensions, stoking the resentment of nonblack citizens who would feel their needs for government assistance were being ignored in a rapidly changing, dislocating economy." If Black Lives Matter and the inequities caused by COVID-19 did not already create a big enough split in our bitterly divided society, said Armstrong Williams, "the continued demand for slavery reparations will finish the job."

Fourth, we can expect a taxpayer revolt. A 2019 Gallup poll found that 67 percent of Americans oppose reparations. A Reuters/Ipsos poll taken in 2020 found that only 20 percent of Americans agreed with the concept of using "taxpayer money to pay damages to descendants of enslaved people in the United States." If reparations are passed, millions will refuse to pay their taxes.

Fifth, reparations would do more harm than good. Shelby Steele argues that reparations would be "facilitating weakness in the very people we're trying to help." Payments would aggravate two chronic problems plaguing the black community—a victim mentality and the unwillingness to accept personal responsibility. Reparations would be self-defeating, Steele said, because entitlements perpetuate a sense of victimization. "The reparations claim is one more attempt to turn African-Americans into victims," agreed David Horowitz. "To focus the social passions of African-Americans on what some Americans may have done to their ancestors fifty or a hundred and fifty years ago is to burden them with a crippling sense of victim-hood."

"[Blacks] are not being held back any more," Steele says. "You can do pretty much anything you want to do in America as a black, including become president." Yet blacks are reluctant to accept personal responsibility. "We want the society to give us more—to be responsible for us," Steele adds. "So when people start to talk about systemic racism built into the system, what they're really doing is expanding the territory of 'entitlement.'"

Retired NFL safety Jack Brewer put the issue in perspective:

"80% of those kids in school can't read and write at proficiency level. So if you're going to talk about reparations, let's talk about reparations through education. Let's actually have reparations that are going to work for the people. I mean, you got a fatherlessness crisis going throughout the state where these black kids are being raised in homes that don't have any dads. And so those are our real issues. Our criminal justice issues, our educational issues. You talk about social justice, it's not going to be completed by just handing out checks to people."

In reality, we have been making reparations for years. "Trillions of dollars in transfer payments have been made to African-Americans in the form of welfare benefits and racial preferences—all under the rationale of redressing historic racial grievances," says David Horowitz." If that is not enough to achieve a "healing," he asks, what will?

Reparations would further isolate blacks from the rest of America. "The reparations claim is one more assault on America, conducted by racial separatists and the political left," says Horowitz. "It is an attack not only on white

Americans, but on all Americans—especially African-Americans."

Once the reparation floodgates are opened, there is no limit to what may be demanded by black activists. "If whites submit to their guilt and beg for penance from the races they have wronged, there's no limit to what the morally superior groups will extract from the now-capitulated oppressor," says Scott Greer. "Especially when that unequal relationship gives them power to make extraordinary demands. The admission of guilt only serves to intensify the grievances of those who feel whites have done them wrong."

For example, some black activists in California say that $5 million per person is not enough. *They want $200 million!*

Denver councilwoman Candi CdeBaca proposed taxing white-owned businesses and redistributing the wealth to minorities. "You could be collecting those extra taxes from White-led businesses all over the city," CdeBaca said, "and redistributing them to Black and Brown owned businesses."

A black woman at Target refused to pay for her purchases, amounting to more than a thousand dollars, on the grounds that she was entitled to them as reparations for what she suffered because of her skin color. The Target store would not accede to her demand, so she assaulted the store manager and had to be restrained by a security guard. Welcome to our brave new world.

Applying Equity to Reparations

Let me conclude with a provocative suggestion. If reparations represent the new face of racial politics, we ought to consider reparations for whites paid for by blacks as compensation for decades of massive violence against the white population.

Black violence has brought the civil society to its knees. Heather Mac Donald has reported the inordinate percentage of all serious crimes that are committed by blacks. "Black crime and violence against whites, gays, women, seniors, young people and lots of others is astronomically out of proportion," said Colin Flaherty in *Don't Make the Black Kids Angry*. As described in Chapter Two, 540,360 felonious assaults were perpetrated by blacks against whites in one three-year period alone.

Whites are suffering from black criminality and anti-white hate in the here and now, not 50-100 years ago. The economic cost to whites and white businesses from black racial violence has amounted to billions. The cost of welfare and other government programs designed to help blacks has amounted to trillions, with very little to show for it.

I am not in favor of any kind of reparations, but if we are going to move in that direction, let's be fair and equitable and give every aggrieved racial and ethnic group a piece of the pie.

A better solution might be not to move in that direction at all. Instead, we can cease government protection of special groups altogether.

About the Author

Ed Brodow is a conservative political commentator, negotiation expert, and bestselling author of ten books including the #1 Amazon Best Seller, *America on its Knees: The Cost of Replacing Trump with Biden.* He has contributed more than 250 articles as a columnist for American Thinker, Newsmax, BizPacReview, Human Events, Townhall, Daily Caller, and other media outlets. An internationally recognized television personality, Ed has appeared on ABC National News, Fox News, GBNews-UK, Inside Edition, CBS, Fortune Business Report, and PBS. He is a former US Marine lieutenant, Fortune 500 sales executive, and Hollywood movie actor. His website is edbrodowpolitics.com. If you want to book Ed for a speaking engagement or media appearance, email ed@brodow.com.

Made in United States
Troutdale, OR
10/02/2023

13323128R00110